Childe Hassam

Childe Hassam

BY DONELSON F. HOOPES

"As the artist practices his peaceful profession, he can hold himself
aloof from the rabble without the least danger or damage to his work. He is alone.
If this is happiness, he has it, as his part in an invisible world, if anyone has it.
He has what the saints sought for in the desert."

Childe Hassam Correspondence,
Papers of the American Academy of Arts and Letters,
Archives of American Art, Smithsonian Institution

WATSON-GUPTILL PUBLICATIONS, NEW YORK

Paperback Edition
First Printing, 1982

1 2 3 4 5 6 7 8 9/86 85 84 83 82

First published 1979 in the United States and Canada by Watson-Guptill Publications,
a division of Billboard Publications, Inc.,
1515 Broadway, New York, N.Y. 10036

Library of Congress Catalog Card Number: 79–15232
ISBN 0-8230-0622-0
ISBN 0-8230-0621-2 pbk.

Manufactured in Japan.

Front cover: *Crystal Palace, Chicago Exposition*
    Coe Kerr Gallery, New York, N.Y.
    (Collection of Mrs. Norman B. Woolworth)

In the preparation of this volume, I have turned to a number of individuals for assistance. I am especially indebted to the following for their gracious responses to my many queries about the life and works of Childe Hassam: Marjorie Henry, Akron Art Institute; Theodore E. Stebbins, Jr., Museum of Fine Arts, Boston; Denny Carter, Cincinnati Art Museum; Kathleen A. Pyne, the Detroit Institute of Arts; Eleanor Radcliffe, Freer Art Gallery; Ethel Moore, University of Georgia, Museum of Art; Gudmund Vigtel and Joel Sturdivant, the High Museum of Art, Atlanta; Doreen Burke, the Metropolitan Museum of Art; Helen A. Harrison, the Parrish Art Museum, Southampton; Linda Grimes, Reynolda House Collection, Winston-Salem; Patricia M. Hurley, Museum of Art, Rhode Island School of Design; Betsy B. Jones, Smith College Museum of Art, Northampton; Bertha Saunders, the Mr. and Mrs. John D. Rockefeller III Collection, New York; Patricia J. Whitesides, the Toledo Museum of Art; and Bruce Guenther, Museum of Art, Washington State University, Pullman.

Many other individuals were helpful to me in ways too numerous to particularize; I trust they will accept my sincere thanks without further elaboration. I am very grateful to Dr. Francis Newton, Warren Adelson, Stuart P. Feld, and Robert C. Graham, Jr., for their kind assistance. A number of distinguished collectors of American art consented to have their treasures reproduced in this volume, and I wish to express sincere thanks to them for their courtesy: Mr. and Mrs. Arthur G. Altschul, Ira Koger, Mr. and Mrs. Meyer Potamkin, the late John D. Rockefeller III and Mrs. Rockefeller, and Mrs. Norman Woolworth.

No work of this kind can be accomplished without access to research materials. To any student of American art, the most significant repository of research information is the Archives of American Art, Smithsonian Institution. Through the kindness and many personal favors of the Archives' West Coast Area Director, Dr. Paul Karlstrom, work on the present project was greatly facilitated. I am obliged also to Eleanor Hartman, Los Angeles County Museum of Art, for her assistance in my researches.

Finally, I wish to thank the staff of Watson-Guptill Publications for their care in the handling of the many details concerning this book. Particularly, I wish to thank Judith Ehrlich, Rights Manager; Dorothy Spencer, Senior Editor; and Donald Holden, Editorial Director, who believed in the value of this undertaking from the beginning, and who sustained its author with good humor and encouragement.

D. F. H.
Los Angeles, California
January 1979

Chronology

1859. Born in Dorchester, Massachusetts, October 17.

1870–1874. Attended the Mather School, Dorchester.

1874–1876. Attended Dorchester High School. Left school to work in accounting office of publisher, Little, Brown and Company, Boston.

1876. Apprenticed in shop of a wood engraver, Boston; worked as free-lance illustrator for magazines and book publishers.

1877–1878. Continued as free-lance illustrator; attended evening life class at the Boston Art Club. Briefly enrolled in Lowell Institute; studied under Dr. William Rimmer.

1879. About this time studied painting with I. M. Gaugengigl, Boston.

1883. First trip to Europe: Great Britain, Netherlands, Brittany, Italy, and Spain. Exhibited sixty-seven European watercolors at the gallery of Williams and Everett, Boston. Took studio at 149 Tremont Street, Boston.

1884. Married Kathleen Maude Doane, February 1.

1886. Second European trip, lasting three years. Established studio in Paris, 11 Boulevard Clichy. Studied briefly at Académie Julian under Gustave Boulanger and Jules Lefébvre.

1887. Exhibited at Paris Salon; began to work in Impressionist manner.

1888. Second acceptance to Paris Salon; exhibited also at Internationalen Kunstaustellung, Munich.

1889. Exhibited at Exposition Universelle, Paris; awarded bronze medal. Exhibited at Galerie Georges Petit, Paris. Trip to London. Returned to New York in the fall; established studio at 95 Fifth Avenue. Assisted in founding of New York Watercolor Club; elected its first president. Exhibited fourteen pastels, sixteen watercolors at Doll and Richards's Gallery, Boston.

1890. Joined Pastel Society, New York; exhibited in the Society's final show. Summer painting trip to New England; visited Gloucester, Massachusetts, and Isles of Shoals. Exhibited at Society of American Artists, New York.

1891. Exhibited four watercolors at Art Institute of Chicago.

1892. Moved studio to Chelsea Hotel, West 23rd Street, New York. Made illustrations for Howells's *Venetian Life*. Summer painting trip to Appledore, Isles of Shoals. Bronze medal, Munich.

1893. Established studio at 152 West 57th Street, New York. Exhibited six oils, four watercolors at World's Columbian Exposition, Chicago; awarded prize in painting.

1894. Summer painting trip to Isles of Shoals. Illustrated *An Island Garden* by Celia Thaxter.

1895. Trip to Havana, Cuba, January. Awarded Webb Prize, 17th Annual Exhibition, Society of American Artists, National Academy of Design, for *Place Centrale and Fort Cabanas, Havana*.

1896. Received prize for painting from Boston Art Club.

1897. Third European trip; visited Italy (Naples, Rome, and Florence), France (Paris and Pont Aven, Brittany), and London. Resigned from Society of American Artists. Founded Ten American Painters group with J. H. Twachtman and J. A. Weir; other members included F. W. Benson, J. R. De Camp, T. W. Dewing, W. L. Metcalf, R. Reid, E. E. Simmons, and E. C. Tarbell. Elected to membership in Lotos Club, New York.

1898. First exhibition of Ten American Painters at Galerie Durand-Ruel, New York, March 31 to April 16. Subsequent exhibition of the Ten at St. Botolph Club, Boston. Hassam taught at Art Students League, New York. Summer at Isles of Shoals.

1899. Awarded Temple Gold Medal, Pennsylvania Academy of the Fine Arts, 68th Annual Exhibition. Summer painting trip to Gloucester, Massachusetts, and Isles of Shoals.

1900. Awarded silver medal, Exposition Universelle, Paris. Summer painting trip to Provincetown, Massachusetts.

1901. Received gold medal, Department of Fine Arts, Pan-American Exposition, Buffalo, New York. Summer at Newport, Rhode Island, and Isles of Shoals.

1902. Elected Associate, National Academy of Design, New York. Summer at New Canaan, Connecticut. About this time took an apartment studio at 27 West 67th Street, New York.

1903. Visited Old Lyme, Connecticut, July, Isles of Shoals, August.

1904. Awarded gold medal, Department of Fine Arts, Universal Exposition St. Louis. Summer at Old Lyme.

1905. Held first one-man exhibition at Montross Gallery, New York; continued to exhibit there annually except for 1921 and 1931. Summer at Old Lyme.

1906. Elected Academician, National Academy of Design, New York; awarded Carnegie Prize, National Academy of Design. Summer at Old Lyme, N.H., and Isles of Shoals.

1908. Trip to the West Coast; visited San Francisco and Portland, Oregon. Painted mural decorations for home of Col. C. E. S. Wood in Portland. Trip to Harney Desert, Oregon.

1909. Summer painting trip to East Hampton, Long Island; Gloucester; Isles of Shoals.

1910. Fourth and last trip to Europe. Worked in Paris and Grez, France; visited Ronda and Toledo, Spain. Received Sesnan Gold Medal, Pennsylvania Academy of the Fine Arts, 105th Annual Exhibition; 3rd Clark Prize, Corcoran Gallery of Art, Washington, D.C., 3rd Biennial Exhibition.

1911. Summer painting trip to Isles of Shoals.

1912. Awarded 1st Clark Prize, Corcoran Gallery of Art, Washington, D.C., 4th Biennial Exhibition; exhibited at American Watercolor Society, New York, 45th Annual Exhibition.

1913. Exhibited at International Exhibition of Modern Art, New York (the Armory Show); represented by six oils, five pastels, one drawing.

1914. Trip to California; visited the Panama–Pacific International Exposition, San Francisco. Hassam is one of twelve American artists honored with exhibitions of their work at the Exposition's Palace of Fine Arts. Painted at Carmel.

1915. Summer at Cos Cob, Connecticut; resumed serious interest in etching. Exhibited seventy-five etchings and drypoints at Frederick Keppel and Co., New York, in fall. Awarded gold medal, Philadelphia Art Club.

1916. Exhibited fifty-nine etchings was well as a group of drawings and watercolors at Frederick Keppel and Co., New York. Extensive showing of work at St. Botolph Club, Boston; Memorial Art Gallery, Rochester, Albright Art Gallery, Buffalo.

1917. Began series of paintings of Fifth Avenue, New York—the *Flag Series.* Began to work in lithography. Large-scale exhibitions mounted at Art Institute of Chicago; Worcester Art Museum, Worcester, Massachusetts; City Art Museum of St. Louis. Summer painting trip to East Hampton.

1918. Final exhibition of Ten American Painters at Montross Gallery, New York. Exhibited *Flag Series* paintings at Galerie Durand-Ruel, New York, November. Awarded Altman Prize, National Academy of Design, New York. Summer painting trips to East Hampton, Gloucester.

1919. Major retrospective exhibition of paintings covering the period 1888–1919 held at William Macbeth Gallery, New York. Milch Gallery, New York becomes his principal dealer; Hassam's work shown in Milch exhibitions, spring and fall. Exhibition of graphic works at Museum of History and Art, Los Angeles.

1920. About this time relocated studio to 130 West 57th Street. Elected to American Academy of Arts and Letters, New York. Established summer home and studio at East Hampton; becomes his permanent summer address.

1922. *Flag Series* given a special exhibition at Corcoran Gallery of Art, Washington, D.C., February.

1923. Exhibited graphic work and paintings at several New York galleries: Milch, Macbeth, Keppel, Scott, and Fowles.

1924. Exhibited etchings at Milwaukee Art Institute.

1925. Publication of book, *Etchings and Drypoints by Childe Hassam*, by Scribner's. Exhibited "classical" subjects at Macbeth Gallery, New York. Exhibition of paintings at Phillips Memorial Art Gallery, Washington, D.C.

1926. Retrospective exhibition at Durand-Ruel, New York, January. Awarded 1st Altman Prize, National Academy of Design, New York; Gold Medal, Department of Fine Arts, Philadelphia Sesqui-Centennial Exposition.

1927. Final trip to California; visits Los Angeles. Given one-man exhibition at American Academy of Arts and Letters, New York, April.

1928. Exhibition of etchings at Museum of Fine Arts, Syracuse.

1929. Paintings shown at California Palace of the Legion of Honor, San Francisco, January; retrospective at Albright Art Gallery, Buffalo, March.

1931. Awarded Pennell Memorial Gold Medal for Etching, Pennsylvania Academy of the Fine arts.

1932. Drawings shown at Carnegie Institute, Pittsburgh, February.

1933. Publication of the complete illustrated catalogue raisonné of Hassam's etchings and drypoints by Leonard Clayton Gallery, New York.

1934. Given Gold Medal for Distinguished Services to the Fine Arts by Association of American Art Dealers, New York.

1935. Died, East Hampton, August 27. Received Saltus Medal for Merit, National Academy of Design. Posthumous exhibition of Hassam's paintings at Milch Gallery, New York, October.

1936. Hassam Fund formally instituted by American Academy of Arts and Letters, New York, November 12.

List of Plates

Childe Hassam

CHILDE HASSAM was one of those fortunate artists to whom the physical act of painting was as natural as breathing and, seemingly, just as essential to life itself. Because of the extraordinary number of works he produced, any attempt to catalogue them completely seems almost impossible. One may say of Hassam, as it was said of Renoir, that he created paintings with the same relentlessness that an apple tree produces apples. With such inspirational abundance, like Renoir's, his works are uneven in quality. Indeed, in the kind of generative drive of creation that marked Hassam's long career, there lay the inevitable opportunity for failure. This is to be noted especially in some of the paintings from the last decade of his life, when a certain preference for sentimental subject matter, combined with a mechanical and somewhat flawed technique, diminished the former vigor of his art. One is tempted to wish that he had exercised a greater discrimination, leaving to posterity only the gems of his fertile talent. But it is doubtful that he ever destroyed any of the bad "apples" from the harvest of his career. The record of Hassam's bequest to the American Academy of Arts and Letters reveals that three hundred oil paintings, ninety-two watercolors, and thirty pastels were conveyed to that institution at his death in 1935. These works were as varied in their quality as they were in subject matter, and represented not only some of Hassam's favorite—and, therefore, unsold—pictures, but also the "leavings." To alter in any significant way the evidence of his life's work would have been antithetical to Hassam's true character.

Forty years have passed since the publication of the last monograph on Hassam, other than those directly related to exhibition catalogues. Of the major figures who comprised the Ten American Painters group, sometimes described as "a kind of academy of American Impressionism," Hassam has remained a respectable but somehow unpopular subject for the biographer. Hassam's *oeuvre* proclaims a passionate attachment to a world of light and beneficence—an attitude no longer valued in our more cynical age. His work is also firmly associated with the much-scorned "genteel tradition" in American art, a phase of our national cultural heritage that evokes little sympathy among modern critics. Yet, the critical neglect of Hassam's career is not due to his having been forgotten; no history of American art published in this century has omitted mention of his name. Indeed, most recent writers on the subject have singled him out as the one American artist whose work most faithfully incorporates the spirit of French Impressionism. Unfortunately, rather than to enhance his reputation, this has served to stigmatize his work more severely than that of his colleagues of the Ten.

"What is American in American Art?" has been a recurrent question in the critical literature, reflecting a chauvinism wrongly applied to art. This criticism has sought to define characteristics unique to American art; and to those critics who find justification in it, Hassam fails the test, for he committed the sin of too closely adhering to a foreign idiom in art. Perhaps the most cogent argument concerning the criteria by which traditional American art should be judged in relation to its European origins asks that American art be defined not so much by the forms it has taken as by the presence of certain qualities that run through its history. As Barbara Novak has pointed out, "What makes [those qualities] indigenous is not their uniqueness to America but rather the frequency or constancy of their occurrence within continuing American traditions to which they also contribute."

Like his fellow American Impressionists, Hassam tended to retain the identity of the subject he painted, instead of dissolving it in an envelope of color in the way of some of the French painters, for example, Claude Monet. In this, he was following a very strong American tradition to particularize and to heighten the reality of the physical world through the painted image. For it must be noted that the American landscape painter of the early 19th century had evolved an approach to rendering nature that deliberately sought for qualities exemplifying the American scene. This approach is called Luminism, and its preoccupation with atmospheric effects in painting prefigured Impressionism by several decades. Luminism is a collective term for the style of a group of American landscape painters born in the first quarter of the 19th century, who engaged in a common pursuit—the search for the artistic equivalent of the light of nature. In so doing, they also raised representational art to new heights of descriptive realism. American Impressionism held on to its realist origins, rather than abandoning them. Thus, as a movement, it did not serve as a portal to modernism, in contrast to its French counterpart, but it was still a reaffirmation of conservative values.

FREDERICK CHILDE HASSAM was born in Dorchester, Massachusetts, in 1859. The family name evolved from that of his ancestor, William Horsham, who settled in Salem in the early 1600s. By the next century, the spelling had changed to "Hasham," and appeared in its ultimate form sometime late in the Colonial era. Early in his life, Hassam showed a preference for his second name, which honored an uncle, and soon took to signing his youthful works "F. Childe Hassam." Hassam regarded both branches of his family with pride: his mother, Rose Hathorn, was related to the novelist Nathaniel Hawthorne (who altered the spelling for effect), and, through his paternal grandfather, Hassam was related to the Hunts, who produced the painter William Morris Hunt and the architect Richard Morris Hunt. These artistic and literary forebears were balanced in the Hassam genealogy by men of action, sea captains, and Revolutionary War patriots. Recounting his life, Hassam noted,

> None of my ancestors became really respectable, for none of them became clergymen, but they always fought in every war (when not sailing the seven seas) for human liberty. Ste-

ven Hassam, aged 16, was a powder boy at Bunker Hill, and lived to bury a son who was killed at Malvern Hill in our Civil War.

The Dorchester of Hassam's youth was not the blighted urban appendage to Boston that it is today, but a prosperous suburban community, respectable and solidly middle class. Young Hassam was educated at the town's Meeting House Hill School, and went on to attend Dorchester High. There he combined a curriculum that included Greek, Latin, French, and German with a program of sports, including boxing and swimming. Hassam did not finish high school. In 1876, after his second year, he took a job in the accounting department of the Boston publishing house of Little, Brown and Company. Very likely, this was the direct result of his family's loss of their modest fortune four years earlier. Frederick Hassam's hardware business in downtown Boston perished in the great fire of 1872, which "in the area between Summer and Pearl Streets from Washington Street to the harbor ... destroyed Trinity Church, burned out the *Transcript* and *Pilot* newspaper offices and devastated many stores, business blocks and warehouses."[1] As the eldest son, the young Hassam recognized his responsibility to contribute to the family income; but at fifteen he was not adept enough for the world of commerce, and so, quickly departed Little, Brown for more suitable employment as an artist.

As a child, Hassam had shown a keen interest in making little pictures in watercolors. He remembered copying the sporting prints in the billiard room of the family house on Olney Street, and using an old horse coach parked in the back yard for a studio. His first recollection of an original work of art, other than his own, was that of Thomas Hewes Hinckley, the painter of sentimental animal subjects, who lived in the nearby town of Milton. Thus, when his supervisor at Little, Brown noted Hassam's facility at drawing, it was suggested that he turn to a career in art. Acting on that advice, Hassam applied for a position as apprentice to a wood engraver, George E. Johnston. Starting with the most menial tasks in the shop, Hassam advanced by learning and mastering each step in the operations, from the machine finishing of the boxwood blocks to the engraving process itself. His talent for drawing assured his rapid rise to staff artist, with responsibility for producing the original designs translated into the wood engravings used by the printers. These projects were commercial assignments, such as designs for newspaper mastheads and business stationery. This early experience gave him a special regard for the graphic media that he carried throughout his life. Hassam took a certain pride in the fact that the masthead for the Marblehead *Messenger,* which he designed in 1876, was still in use by that newspaper fifty years later.

Having learned the rudiments of engraving under Johnston, Hassam found opportunities for creative work elsewhere. As freelance illustrator, he was on the threshold of a career in an emerging branch of American art. For over a decade, Winslow Homer's designs had adorned many of the covers of *Harper's Weekly,* while the younger Edwin Austin Abbey was raising the illustrator's art to new levels of excellence within the pages of that same "journal of civil-

ization." During the golden age of American illustration, the last two decades of the 19th century, Hassam became an important figure in the profession, while at the same time developing a separate career as a painter. In addition to his work in *Harper's,* he produced illustrations for such other periodicals as *The Century* and *Scribner's,* as well as for juvenile publications like *Babyland* and *Saint Nicholas.* Occasionally, he would furnish designs for use as book illustrations; several of his early watercolors were reproduced in color in William Dean Howells's *Venetian Life,* published in 1892. Two years later, Hassam provided the illustrations for *An Island Garden,* the last published work of his friend Celia Laighton Thaxter, the New England poet.

SOMETIME around 1878, Hassam began to take formal lessons in drawing and painting. While continuing to support himself as a free-lance illustrator, he joined the Boston Art Club's evening classes, where he worked directly from a model for the first time and painted portraits and figure studies in oil. In his reminiscences, he particularly mentions one portrait, which he kept throughout his life, "a small canvas, and the head will bear examination with a [magnifying] glass. It is in the spirit of the Dutchmen." This passage is particularly revealing of Hassam's early preference for the new realism that was being championed by the most advanced teachers in Europe. At that very moment, in Munich, Wilhelm Leibl was dispensing the gospel in realism to young Americans, such as William Merritt Chase and Frank Duveneck, while in Paris, Charles Emile Carolus-Duran was providing the same impetus to John Singer Sargent and a host of other budding painters, many of them Americans. This new realism allied itself to the work of Courbet and Manet, and especially looked for inspiration in the works of such 17th-century realist painters as Frans Hals and Diego Velázquez. Followers of the movement sought for a return to more painterly values in art and rejected outworn academic modes. As Axel von Saldern notes, they "studied the Dutch and Spanish masters more carefully than any other realists of the past and employed what they could use—technique, general approach, thematic choice—to make their own paintings more truthful, more convincing, more direct, and aesthetically more subtle."

It is known that Hassam began taking private painting lessons from Ignaz Marcel Gaugengigl, who had recently arrived in Boston from his native Bavaria. It is probably through this artist that the germ of the Munich realist movement was planted in the receptive minds of Hassam and some of his fellow students in the Boston Art Club, where Gaugengigl also taught. In an interview given in 1927, Hassam recalled having been a member of a Paint and Clay Club at this time. It was a small group, composed of perhaps a dozen artists, some of whom became lifelong friends—John B. Johnston, Edward Grant, Marcus Waterman, and Peter Roose. These young painters and sculptors obtained the teaching services of the famous Dr. William Rimmer, the self-taught painter, sculptor, master of anatomical drawing, and sometime doctor of medicine. Hassam had been taking drawing lessons from Rimmer at Boston's Lowell Institute for a few months in 1878, and probably was responsible for induc-

---

[1] Walter Muir Whitehill, Boston, *A Topographical History* (Cambridge: Harvard University Press, 1959), p. 175.

ing the formidable doctor to give private lessons to the members of the Paint and Clay Club. We can see that Hassam subjected himself to an intensive learning program that favored the tutorial method over that of the general art school. Although Boston's Museum of Fine Arts had opened an art school in its new and fashionable Victorian Gothic building on Copley Square, Hassam avoided it.

Of the specific influences upon Hassam's youthful sensibilities little is known. His kinsman, William Morris Hunt, had returned to Boston from Europe in 1862, bringing with him not only paintings by the Barbizon School, but also a missionary's zeal for spreading in America the gospel of this conservative French school of realist painting. Hunt's teachings are recorded in his *Talks on Art,* published in Boston in 1875. The book contains advice on the practice of painting that seems particularly advanced for its time. It is filled with such admonitions to the young artist as "You must sacrifice as many details as possible," "Keep your masses flat, simple and undisturbed," and "It is the impression of the thing you want." We can be sure that Hassam was well acquainted with Hunt's book, and put it to use in his own work. As late as 1924, Hassam retained a vivid memory of his first sight, through Hunt's collection of French art, of what Hassam termed "impressionist painting." Duncan Phillips, in his foreword to the Hassam exhibition at the Macbeth Gallery that year, quotes Hassam in this regard, pointing out that early in his career the artist had been deeply affected by the paintings of the 19th-century Dutchman Johan Barthold Jongkind, one of Hunt's favorites. Thus, about 1878–79, Hassam began to work directly from nature, painting views in and around Boston. With Hunt's Barbizon masters as a guide, he groped his way toward an understanding of light and atmospheric perspective.

Although his most successful efforts at landscape painting were realized after an extended trip to Europe in 1886–89, Hassam acknowledged no particular debt to that experience, so far as his grasp of technique was concerned. He was proud of his youthful independence and initiative, and always resisted assessments of his career that placed undue emphasis on the influence of foreign study. He wrote to his friend Ellery Sedgewick, "I have to debunk the idea that I learned to paint in France. I learned to paint in Boston before I ever went to France." Indeed, Hassam's earliest influences in style and technique were the preimpressionist Barbizon painters and the early 19th-century English watercolorists, whose works he found in Boston. The English watercolorists were crucial in Hassam's development, for though he was just beginning to experiment with oil at this time, Hassam's principal occupation in the late 1870's and early 1880's was with watercolor.

In 1866, the American Water Color Society was founded in New York, under the aegis of the prestigious National Academy of Design, and during the next ten years, the watercolor medium met with increasing critical support. While New York led the way in establishing a forum for the medium, Boston soon saw the birth of its own Society of Water Color Painters. The annual exhibitions of these embryonic American watercolor societies usually contained a selection of works by noted English artists, then regarded as the finest practitioners of the medium. A favorite was Joseph M. W. Turner, the great English landscape painter, who was considered a supreme modern master and served as a model for every aspiring

artist up until about 1880. It is not surprising, then, that some of Hassam's early watercolors so closely follow Turner's manner in the handling of broad, luminous washes; this may be especially noted in Hassam's pure landscape subjects, which are devoid of figurative elements.

Hassam was moderately successful at selling his watercolors at this stage in his career, although it seems he did not acquire a dealer until 1883. And he had gained enough status in Boston to launch into part-time teaching. His watercolor classes included as students Jane Hunt, sister of William Morris Hunt, and Celia Leighton Thaxter, with whom he formed a deep and lasting friendship, although Mrs. Thaxter was twenty-five years his senior. These are the only names definitely connected to Hassam's watercolor classes, and they suggest that his students were only interested amateurs, rather than other young professionals.

IN OCTOBER 1880, Hassam marked his twenty-first birthday. He still lived in the family house in Dorchester, and commuted to downtown Boston, where he found work as an illustrator with the publishing houses and attended painting sessions at the art clubs in the evenings. His life was so circumscribed by work and study that he had not ventured much beyond the confines of the city, despite the fact that the Massachusetts Bay area offered superb scenery for the artist. One of its most celebrated locations is the harbor town of Gloucester on Cape Ann, not forty miles from Boston. This area had been attracting artists since the 1840's and 1850's, when Fitz Hugh Lane lived and worked there; Winslow Homer was painting watercolors there during the summer of Hassam's twenty-first year. In 1882, in the company of his friend the watercolor painter Ross Turner, Hassam visited Gloucester for the first time. There he met Kenyon Cox, an artist from New York. Although Cox was only three years older than Hassam, he had already spent five years in Paris, first at the Ecole des Beaux-Arts under Jean-Léon Gérôme and later in the atelier of Charles Emile Carolus-Duran. This meeting may well have moved Hassam to reassess his ambitions. Whether Cox provided the impetus for his decision to travel abroad the next year is conjecture, but it is certain that in the months following the trip to Gloucester Hassam made an important commitment to a more ambitious career: "I had made money by selling watercolors. Then I made illustrations that were very well paid for.... I said to myself, 'If you're going to paint, let's stop [being an illustrator].' So I stopped."

When the steamship *Anchoria,* bound for Glasgow, cleared Boston Harbor in the spring of 1883, Childe Hassam was aboard. Embarking for Europe meant more than the breaking of home ties. He was also interrupting his courtship of Kathleen Maude Doane, a young woman from Dorchester who had been a family friend for several years. Hassam's sense of dislocation was lessened by the companionship of a fellow member of the Paint and Clay Club, Edmund H. Garrett; together they had planned a tour that would take them to several of the major cities. Landing at Glasgow, they boarded a train for Edinburgh, where Hassam painted his first European watercolors amid the ancient settings of Reed's Close and White Horse Close. Pressing on to London, Hassam and Garrett found a convenient hotel in Cork Street. This was not far from Burlington House, home of the venerable Royal Academy of Arts where exhibitions of contemporary English painting could be seen. At the National Gallery in Trafalgar Square, Hassam sought out the collections of English watercolor painting, while Hogarth's *The Shrimp Girl* seems to have made an indelible impression on him. And at the British Museum, there were more Turners.

Garrett and Hassam crossed the Channel to France. Their progress through Europe that summer can be only incompletely reconstructed by noting the subjects Hassam painted and through reference to his recollections of the trip, which are contained in the Lockman Papers in the Archives of American Art. A beach scene identified as Dunkerque (Hirschl and Adler Galleries, New York) survives, as well as a watercolor identified as *A Landscape with River, Holland* (Hirschl and Adler Galleries, New York). From the Low Countries, where they studied works of the 17th-century masters, their movements become obscure. However, their most likely route lay across northwestern France, perhaps through Switzerland, to Italy. There is no evidence to suggest that Hassam and his friend stopped in Paris. On balance, this seeming lack of interest in the capital of European art is not surprising—Paris had neither museums full of Turners, nor landscape subjects to paint. But Venice promised grand prospects of the Grand Canal, and Turner had painted there. As might be expected, most of Hassam's renditions of that famous cityscape reflect the influence of Turner's glorious works in the British Museum. From Venice, the companions went on to Naples, taking the steamer through the Adriatic rather than proceeding overland. Following a side trip to Florence, they took ship again and landed in Spain where Hassam reported having painted a view of the Alhambra in Granada. Toward fall, they booked passage on a liner bound for New York.

It had been a successful trip. The fate of Garrett's work from that summer is unknown, but Hassam's portfolio was full. From this group of finished and in-progress watercolors, he selected sixty-seven papers for an exhibition at the gallery of Williams and Everett, which opened in Boston late in 1883. It must be assumed that sales from this exhibition went well, for a few months later, on February 1, 1884, Hassam married Kathleen Maude Doane. Maude, as she preferred to be known, would henceforth share in all her husband's struggles and triumphs over the next fifty years. She was not an artist. As Hassam said, "I should call her artistic. . . . She did not paint, but could appreciate art." Never did he paint a formal portrait of her, but a little watercolor of 1889, *Maude Sewing* (Hirschl and Adler Galleries, New York) confirms Adeline Adams's description of her as "a beautiful . . . girl, somewhat younger than himself."

In keeping with his expanding lifestyle, Hassam acquired his first studio, at 149 Tremont Street, opposite Boston Common. His immediate neighbor at 149 Tremont was the sixty-year-old George Fuller, who had returned to Boston from Deerfield in 1877, following an unsuccessful venture at farming. Fuller had resumed his interrupted career as a painter, and was working in a style that echoed Hunt's enthusiasm for the Barbizon School. A contemporary writer, Charles Caffin, describes Fuller's work as "immersed in atmosphere, tenderly elusive, quietly luminous, a revery of color,

reticently harmonious." These words can also be applied to the paintings Hassam completed in the period 1884–86, and are an especially apt description of his *Boston Common at Twilight* (Plate 2). In effect, Hassam was committing himself to the tenets of tonalism, that manifestation in late 19th-century American painting which, as an outgrowth of the Barbizon School, sought a painterly and romantic view of nature. Fuller was one of the foremost exponents of tonalism, and Hassam's close proximity to this distinguished older artist could not have failed to stimulate his work in that direction. With ever a canny eye to the realities of the art marketplace, Hassam also acknowledged his admiration for the work of John J. Enneking, whose tonalist canvases made him "New England's highest-priced, most popular landscape painter" between 1878 and 1916.

Hassam's oils of 1884–86 imply a new seriousness of purpose. He now concerned himself almost exclusively with painting the effects of atmosphere. Representation of the human element became a secondary interest in these new pictures, which are essentially poetic statements about the city at twilight, or how it looked on a dull rainy day overhung with leaden skies.

After his début at the Williams and Everett Gallery, Hassam supported himself by selling an occasional painting directly from his studio, thus saving the dealer's commission. At least once he fell back on old resources, when for example, late in 1883, a Boston publisher asked him to provide illustrations for *The High Tide on the Coast of Lincolnshire* by Jean Ingelow, Hassam agreed. For this project Hassam employed sketches from his recent trip, proving that between his visits to Edinburgh and London, he had seen the famous North Sea coast and its celebrated artists' colonies. But Hassam seems to have been intent upon making his mark in Boston as a painter in oils, and even though the Boston *Globe* took favorable notice of his watercolors at Williams and Everett, that appears to have been the only public appreciation of his work during the period 1883–86. Meanwhile, his acquaintances among the artist community of Boston had enlarged to include Emil Carlsen, Abbott Graves, Edmund Tarbell, and Frank Benson. By 1884, each one of these men had studied in Paris, and, doubtless, they shared their experiences with Hassam. The decade of the 1880's marked the high tide of the flood of young American artists seeking to better their careers in Paris. As the critic Henry James noted at the time, "When today we look for 'American Art' we find it mainly in Paris. When we find it out of Paris, we at least find a good deal of Paris in it." Hassam had worked diligently for two years following his first European trip, without marked improvement in his circumstances. Perhaps Paris would offer the key to the kind of success he longed for. Thus, in the spring of 1886, he gave up his studio on Tremont Street, and with Maude, departed again for Europe.

The young couple declined the Bohemian existence typical of most new arrivals. They looked around the Left Bank *quartiers*, but found the Montmartre section on the other side of the Seine more to their liking, and so took a lease on a spacious apartment with attached studio at 11 Boulevard Clichy, not far from the Place Pigalle. As Hassam was proud to point out, "We were living in quarters just as any French painter would who had 'arrived.' We had a French maid." Although not quite thirty, Hassam obviously saw himself as an experienced artist, and not as an art student. Consequently, he wanted his lifestyle to reflect that image, even though the two could have lived far more cheaply in Montparnasse. Armed with a letter of introduction from Albert E. Munsell, the color theorist, Hassam gained immediate entry to the famous Académie Julian, where, he noted, he "mostly drew from life." Julian's, a privately run school, was presided over by the critics Gustave Boulanger and Jules Lefébvre. It was considered equal to the government-sponsored Ecole des Beaux-Arts, in terms of the thoroughness with which it prepared its students in the disciplines of drawing and pictorial composition. Especially in the 1880's, Julian's became a *locus operandi* for scores of young Americans, many of whom would become close associates of Hassam in the years ahead. Some of those who had already studied under Boulanger and Lefebvre were John H. Twachtman, Edward Simmons, Thomas W. Dewing, and Willard Metcalf. Robert Reid came to study there at about the same time as Hassam, and they struck up a lifelong friendship. Shortly after Hassam arrived in Paris, he met the painter Gari Melchers, then living in Holland, who had come to the city to accept an honorable mention in the Salon of 1886. And the next year, when his own picture, *Une Averse, Rue Bonaparte* (Plate 3), was shown at the Salon, Hassam met Frank Boggs, who was also occupying a studio apartment at 11 Boulevard Clichy. Henry James might well have added to his observations that one could also find American *artists* mainly in Paris in the decade of the 1880's.

ᛗANY American artists went to Paris during the 1880's because they were attracted by the new mode of painting called Impressionism, which had burst upon the public consciousness in 1874. Meteorlike, it had flashed across the Paris art scene, and in only a few years had completely achieved its aims. The year 1886 witnessed the almost simultaneous openings of the eighth, and last, exhibition of the original Impressionist group in Paris and a massive display of French Impressionist paintings in New York, the latter sponsored by the master impresario of modern French art, Paul Durand-Ruel. The three hundred works shown in New York included paintings by Mary Cassatt, the American painter who had become the standard-bearer for Impressionism in the United States, and by her French colleagues, Manet, Degas, Monet, Morisot, Pissarro, Renior, and Sisley, among others. The American exhibition found immediate and widespread critical approval, quite unlike the reception attending the official birth of the Impressionist movement in Paris twelve years before. Durand-Ruel had taken care to leaven the exhibition with works by some of the Barbizon painters, who were already well known and accepted in America, but there is, perhaps, a more substantive explanation for the success of the New York show. The ground had been already thoroughly prepared through the efforts of influential painter-teachers, such as William Merritt Chase, and those in the position to lend the necessary prestige of institutional approval, like John F. Weir, director of the Yale University School of Fine Arts.

Hassam's motives for going to Paris undoubtedly involved a keen interest in what the Impressionists were doing, but they went beyond that to his recognition of the need for refining his talent in the larger crucible of contemporary art. He did not change his style of painting substantially during his first year there, but a subtle shift away from his drier Boston manner was made by the spring of 1887, as he started to employ a more painterly brushwork. A comparison between *Une Averse, Rue Bonaparte* (Plate 3) of that year and *Rainy Day, Boston* (Plate 1) of 1885 reveals strong continuities, especially in the deep perspective in the two compositions and the marked similarities of moody atmospheric effects. The Paris subject is, in effect, only a variation on a familiar theme rather than a new departure, and speaks of his cautiousness about assimilating new influences. However, in 1887, Hassam also produced *Le Jour du Grand Prix* (Plate 4), a picture that abruptly proclaimed his entry into the ranks of the Impressionists. With its blond palette, flickering brush strokes, and brilliant *plein air* light, the Grand Prix subject seems almost a thing done to test his abilities against the best efforts of his older French contemporaries. Incontestably, he succeeded in creating a painting that is the epitome of the Impressionist style, but Hassam consistently rejected this classification. As he observed in a letter to his friend Ellery Sedgewick, "everybody who paints and sees is probably an 'impressionist,' but none of those men who are supposed to have painted with dots and dashes ever really did do just that." If the search for the equivalent in paint of the light of nature involved borrowing some of the Impressionists' innovations, then he borrowed, but at no time in his career did Hassam subordinate the emotional content of the represented image to the supremacy of color or technique. Indeed, most of the paintings from those Paris years also tell of his search for a synthesis of his commitment to realism and the demands of a viable plastic expression. For this reason, his Paris pictures tend to shift about in style, sometimes emphasizing objective realism, and at other times concentrating on the decorative qualities of the painted surface.

This may be noted particularly in his work from 1888, when he oscillated between the realism of *Chez la Fleuriste* (Chrysler Museum, Norfolk) and the decorative qualities of *April Showers, Champs Elysées, Paris* (Joslyn Art Museum, Omaha). These paintings were not mere experiments, however, even though Hassam had not settled down to a consistent style. For example, *Le Crépuscule* (Hammer Galleries, New York), a large canvas that combines the two tendencies somewhat to the detriment of both, was submitted to at least three major exhibitions: the Exposition Universelle, 1889, Paris; the Pennsylvania Academy of the Fine Arts Annual Exhibition, 1890, Philadelphia; and the Internationalen Kunstaustellung, 1892, Munich. It must be assumed that Hassam regarded this painting as a creditable example of his work, despite its conceptual variance with the bulk of his output at this time.

ᛈARIS was Hassam's world for three years. Except for an occasional visit with friends who lived at Villiers-le-Bel, some ten miles north of the city, Hassam made no effort to travel. He showed no interest in seeing Barbizon or even Giverny, where the celebrated Claude Monet lived and welcomed many American visitors, such as his painter-disciple Theodore Robinson, who traveled to Paris in 1887. This does not necessarily imply a lack of intellectual curiosity, but was most likely the result of the financial pressures of maintaining the grandeur of his chosen lifestyle and the responsibilities of marriage. In order to afford all of this, Hassam's time must have been almost completely given over to work. Scrapbook clippings he kept include a notice published in the Boston *Advertiser,* in 1887, for a public sale of 120 of his works, while a year later, the same newspaper mentioned an exhibition sale of 35 of his paintings at the gallery of Noyes, Cobb and Company of Boston. In 1889, Hassam exhibited works for sale in Paris at the Galerie Georges Petit, as well as in Boston at Doll and Richards, the prestigious dealers who also represented Winslow Homer. All of these ventures called for much planning and effort, especially the Boston shows, which required the transoceanic shipment of his works from Paris. In the meantime, Hassam also worked toward achieving critical notice, and submitted paintings to the Paris Salon exhibitions of 1887, 1888, and 1889. In 1889, he captured a bronze medal at the Exposition Universelle.

Hassam had enjoyed the best that Paris could offer, both in terms of its sophisticated ambience and its material and critical rewards. He had worked hard to forge a place for himself, and it was now time to return home. The apartment at 11 Boulevard Clichy was vacated, and while preparing their departure from Paris, the Hassams sublet temporary quarters on the nearby Boulevard Rochechouart. The new apartment had been occupied by an artist who had left some of his paintings behind. As if in a revelation, Hassam came to a clearer understanding of the direction he had been seeking for three years: "I looked at these experiments in pure color and saw it was what I was trying to do." Almost at once his art found the cohesion it had thus far lacked. After a final visit to friends at Villiers-le-Bel in the summer of 1889, the Hassams left Paris, spent a few weeks in London, and then boarded ship for the United States. Hassam's birthday, the 17th of October, was celebrated at sea—he was thirty now and had finally "arrived."

Boston always had been receptive to Hassam's art, and it was there that he held his first exhibition of the new season. For two weeks in mid-November 1889, Doll and Richards' Gallery on Park Street displayed a group of nineteen pastels and sixteen watercolors of mostly European subjects. Hassam had begun to use the pastel medium in Paris. His Longchamps race meeting scenes of the Grand Prix share Degas's love of the elegance of the *beau monde* who frequented these events, but Hassam concentrated on the human spectacle rather than the sport (see Plate 5). Many of the new watercolors were views of the English seaside resort of Broadstairs and cheerful prospects of London's Hyde Park. A reviewer for the Boston *Transcript* proclaimed that this latest showing was "one of those happy and spontaneous displays which gives pleasure by their own cheerful character and vivacity, their youthful dash and pure gaiety . . . a gusto on the part of the artist who convinces his public by every crayon stroke that it is a fine thing to be a painter. . . ."

This was an auspicious homecoming, but Hassam already had determined to take up residence in New York. By December 1889, he and Maude were installed in a studio apartment at 95 Fifth Avenue. It must have been a comfortable transition from Paris. A few steps from their door south on Fifth Avenue lay Washington Square, bordered by elegant brownstone townhouses and dominated by Stanford White's newly erected ceremonial arch, so reminiscent of its more famous counterpart on the Champs Elysées. Bruce Crane, whose tonalist landscape paintings had just earned him an Associate membership in the National Academy of Design, was also an occupant of number 95. A friendship developed between the two artists, although the gregarious Hassam felt disquieted by his neighbor's introspective personality.

Hassam was a doer and a joiner; he relished the chummy world of artists' societies, and plunged into it with enormous enthusiasm. Immediately upon his arrival he helped found the New York Watercolor Club. Because of his leadership in pressing for an organization that would be more open to women members than was the existing American Water Color Society, he was elected as the Club's first president. Significantly, their initial meeting was held in the studio of a woman artist, Julia Baker. The Club held its first exhibition at the American Art Galleries on Madison Square, where Durand-Ruel had presented his Impressionist group just four years before. When the Society of American Painters in Pastel asked Hassam to join in 1890, his work was singled out for special praise. This was a high mark for one of the newest members of a Society whose roster included older artists such as William Merritt Chase and John H. Twachtman. The year 1890 also brought Hassam an invitation to join the Players Club, a gathering place for artists and actors on Gramercy Square that had been founded by the eminent Edwin Booth. But he had to wait twelve years before being inducted into the nation's most prestigious art organization, the National Academy of Design. That honor required his resignation from the Academy's rebellious secessionist group, the Society of American Artists, in which Hassam held a membership until 1898. This network of contacts created the underpinnings of a successful career at a time when dealers played only a minor role in establishing artists' reputations. Hassam's inherent sociability served him well in this respect.

I
T IS the consensus of most historians that Hassam's paintings of the 1890's are his finest achievements. While it would be false to deny the excellence of many of his later works, this judgement is generally accurate. In the nineties and the early years of the new century, his approach was more painterly, in the sense that his primary concern was light and color. He had gradually abandoned tonalism during his years in Paris, and had brought his art to accommodate the tenets of Impressionism in a way that suggests evolution rather than an abrupt change for the sake of fashion. Adeline Adams, who knew him, wrote that he was "never the man to do things because others were doing it . . . it was in his character to weigh [Impressionism] for its principles, not for its . . . personages." By 1890, he was demonstrating already that Impressionism was a truly international movement. If Monet could take an ordinary street scene on the Boulevard des Capucines and make an interesting painting of it, so could Hassam paint New York's Union Square, and thereby defy Charles Eliot Norton's lament that "in America even the shadows are ugly." Indeed, if one were to judge New York in this decade solely on the basis of Hassam's lambent paintings of its principal ornaments—Central Park, Madison

Square, Union Square, and Washington Square—it would have appeared to be the most beautiful city on earth. It has been the conventional wisdom that Hassam's "paintings were not rigorous studies of light, but delightful evocations of well-liked places."[2] To be sure, Hassam did not dissolve his subjects into the kind of brilliant broken color Monet employed, but neither are his scenes of New York merely topographical. As with the best of the period's French Impressionism, Hassam's paintings are primarily about *painting,* the organization of form and space in terms of pigment.

The assertion that American Impressionism had little more to offer than provincial charm is nowhere more abundantly refuted than in the work Hassam produced at Appledore, one of a small group of islands off the New Hampshire coast. Over a twenty-year period, beginning in the summer of 1890, he created a series of paintings that invites comparison with the work of the best of the *plein air* Frenchmen. The Appledore subjects possess a conviction and palpability of light and atmosphere that transformed this unremarkable little island into an American Etretat.

The pattern of activity Hassam established soon after his arrival in New York would remain constant for most of his life, with summers spent painting in New England and winters working in his studio in the city. There were periods, of course, when he traveled abroad or in the West; and in his later years, as his career became centered in New York, Long Island eventually replaced Appledore for summer painting. Hassam loved his adopted city, the amiable society of its artists and writers, its fabulous personalities and glittering celebrities.

The Hassams did not remain long in their Fifth Avenue apartment. New York's growth pattern was moving gradually uptown; even the famed 10th Street studio building was losing its long-time occupants to the general exodus. In 1895, William Merritt Chase, noted painter and teacher and one of its more colorful denizens, migrated north to more commodious quarters on Stuyvesant Square. In 1892, the Hassams took a suite at the Chelsea Hotel on West 23rd Street, a haven long favored by artists and writers, and the following year they removed to a studio apartment building named the Rembrandt at 152 West 57th Street, two blocks south of Central Park. It was an impressive location for a studio, since 57th Street was fast becoming the city's cultural center. In 1892, the Art Students League opened its new building at number 215, and concert-goers attended the inaugural performance at Carnegie Hall. Just to the east on Fifth Avenue, a spectacular parade of Renaissance palaces, built for newly minted millionaires, made its stately way past Central Park's Plaza corner. At that site, in 1895, Richard Morris Hunt, architect brother of the painter William Morris Hunt, erected an enormous 16th-century-style French château for Cornelius Vanderbilt II. Vanderbilt's daughter, Gertrude, was twenty at the time and dreamed of being a sculptor, an unlikely ambition for a princess of New York's Four Hundred. But, then, as S. C. Burchell put it, "there is an elegance of spirit which has never left the Avenue, an elegance of spirit generating—most particularly on late spring afternoons in the vicinity of the Plaza Hotel—the feeling that anything is possible." Hassam rode the crest of this era of opulence

and euphoria; his art spoke of a world of beauty and order, and he found a ready audience for it. In 1892, he exhibited at the Internationalen Kunstaustellung in Munich, and the following year, at the World's Columbian Exposition in Chicago. There he was represented by four watercolors and six oils, which were hung in the Fine Arts Department's grandiose Beaux Arts pavilion at the White City, as the exposition complex was called. On both occasions, Hassam's work earned him medals, those fusty, 19th-century marks of official recognition. From then on, he garnered prizes almost every year from both foreign and American sponsors of prestigious exhibitions—Hassam had become a successful painter.

THE SUMMER of 1894 was one of artistic triumph and personal tragedy for him, and seemed to usher in a new phase of his career. His command of the oil medium had fully matured; he produced sumptuous impastos and liquid transparencies of color that seem effortlessly to convey every nuance his eye beheld. His masterpiece of that summer, *The Room of Flowers* (Plate 9), breathes a life that makes more poignant the knowledge that its subject, Celia Thaxter, died shortly after its completion. Hassam and his friend, the painter J. Appleton Brown, attended her burial in the garden she had celebrated in poem and prose and had tended so carefully at the little house on Appledore. He would not return to the island for several years. Perhaps the place carried too many associations—not only had he lost a friend, but his kinsman, William Morris Hunt, also died there, fifteen years before, an apparent suicide. For whatever reason, in 1895, Hassam decided upon a complete change of scene. Leaving Maude in New York, he took an ocean voyage to Cuba in the company of a businessman and remained there for about a month. Late the following year he embarked on an extensive tour abroad, visiting familiar places in London, Paris, Naples, and Rome. He returned to New York in 1897, laden with the results of the full painting schedule he had kept while in Europe. The paintings of this third European trip reveal a new flamboyance of attack, a heightened sense of immediacy that conveys a life and movement never before so fully realized in his work.

This restlessness and vitality also began to lead him toward a more independent position in the New York art world. He felt encumbered by the methods employed by the management of some of the large exhibitions, particularly that of the Society of American Artists. The Society had been formed in 1877 in response to a temporary breakdown in the leadership of the National Academy of Design. Caught in the general economic crisis of the 1870's, the Academy was forced to close its school for two seasons. This prompted the students to establish their own facilities, the Art Students League. The Society of American Artists was the exhibition arm of the League. By the time Hassam decided to become independent, the Society's activities were increasingly being hosted by the Academy, which subsumed it entirely by 1906. The Society's annual exhibitions tended to follow the Academy's established mode—the display of as many paintings as possible in a given space, generally without regard for the frequently chaotic juxtapositions that resulted. Hassam felt this approach was both archaic and

---

[2] Oliver W. Larkin, *Art and Life in America* (New York: Rhinehart, 1956), p. 304.

unesthetic. And on a very practical level, the Academy's shows did not attract many clients; its annual exhibitions, and those of the Society as well, were geared to a system of prizes and honors rather than to sales. Not surprisingly, Hassam found others who felt as he did, and was supported immediately by J. Alden Weir and John H. Twachtman.

At a meeting in New York on December 17, 1897, ten artists came together to sign their names to two documents. The first was a formal testament of resignation from the Society; the second specified the simplified rules the new organization would live by:

> We the undersigned agree to co-operate and consolidate for the purpose of holding an annual exhibition of work, each member pledging himself to exhibit, and we moreover agree to admit no other man to this group without an unanimous consent.

In addition to the three founding members, Hassam, Weir, and Twachtman, there were Willard L. Metcalf, Thomas W. Dewing, Edward E. Simmons, Frank W. Benson, Edmund C. Tarbell, and Joseph R. De Camp. All but De Camp had studied in Paris during the heyday of French Impressionism. Unquestionably, they all owed an allegiance to the spirit of modern French painting, but none except Hassam showed more than slight adherence to its *plein air* methods. Rather than being a tightly knit group, the Ten, as they came to be known, reveal the great diversity of style and subject matter that constituted American Impressionism. Hassam, Weir, Twachtman, and Metcalf are strongest in their claim to be called Impressionists, since they were foremost in their use of the characteristic blond palette and chose landscape most frequently as their subject matter. Tarbell, Benson, and De Camp were primarily portrait painters. As such, they reverted most often to subject matter associated with the "genteel tradition," one that seems almost antithetical to the spirit of Impressionism. Simmons and Reid spent the major part of their careers as mural painters, a métier not suited to Impressionism, although their few existing easel pictures attest to capable handling of Impressionist technique. And, finally, Dewing must be accounted a practitioner of a kind of reverse Impressionism—that of the diminution of light. Their association imposed no philosophy, but was formed out of motives of friendship, the search for mutual advantage through the pooling of effort, and a shared concern for the state of American art. They were mature, established artists at the time the Ten was formed. Reid was the youngest at thirty-six; Dewing, at forty-seven, the senior member. There was not the slightest hint of rebellion among them.

A S A STYLE, Impressionism had long since become acceptable to American audiences. By 1898, the movement had not only become preeminent and the standard fare to be seen in the large national exhibitions, but it was in danger of losing its vitality by lapsing into a bland and routine mannerism. As spokesman for the Ten, Hassam declared that the group had parted company with the Society of American Artists not over the issue of style, but over the question of esthetics. It was the group's intention to rescue American painting from the degradation, as they saw it, of the monstrous exhibitions staged not only by the Society but the

National Academy as well. Hassam and his colleagues believed in the principles of beauty and good taste as basic to their whole experience as artists. This devotion extended to the manner in which their paintings should be exposed to the public. They frankly allied themselves with the advanced ideas of the Esthetic Movement, which wanted to apply the concepts of oriental design known as *japonisme* to the exhibit of art. The name of James A. M. Whistler was the symbolic standard-bearer behind whom they rallied in an effort to create a purist environment for the exhibition of paintings.

The attempt to establish a "Japanese view," as Hassam called it, was manifested in the Ten's first group show, in March 1898, at the New York gallery of Paul Durand-Ruel, who had been sympathetic to many new ventures. Each artist was represented by a few carefully chosen works—no more than three or four—and each was assigned equal space. Contrary to the accepted method of hanging pictures, only one line of paintings was permitted; they were all hung at eye level, and enhanced by a scrupulously selected wall color. An atmosphere of quiet contemplation reigned, and the contrast with the Academy's galleries must have been almost shocking. What marks the Ten as innovators, besides their rigorous overhaul of exhibition methods, were the procedures under which the group agreed to operate. They permitted no officers, no jury, and no prizes, and, at first, even allowed the exhibitor, Durand-Ruel, to decide how to arrange their pictures.

The Ten continued to exhibit together through the next twenty years, a period that included the brief flourishing of Robert Henri's The Eight, better known by the pejorative term Ashcan School, and the rise of early modernism, marked in the United States by the Armory Show of 1913. The Ten never benefited from the presence on their roster of Theodore Robinson, a most promising Impressionist painter who died in 1896. Nor did Twachtman live long; his untimely death in 1902 halted innovative experiments with color that seemed to presage a fresh approach to Impressionism. Twachtman's place was eventually taken by William Merritt Chase, who, with typical flourish, accepted the Ten's invitation. He wrote,

> My dear Hassam,
> I like to keep good company. I am therefore glad to be one of the number of Ten. It shall be my endeavor to show things as will be in keeping with the kinds of pictures you and your colleagues have shown—and to your credit each year since the society was organized.
>
> Very respectfully
> April 2nd 1905   Wm. M. Chase

Chase's authoritative style, both as a painter and as a personality, helped bolster the cause of the Ten's conservative art expression in a world in rapid transition. But the course of modern art was moving swiftly against them. Even at the beginning of their association, critics had registered surprise, even disappointment, that the Ten harbored no "revolutionists" in their midst. By 1915, a writer for *American Art News*, James Britten, predicted the demise of the group through "inanition which is bound to result from a lapse of public interest." The Ten ended their association quietly three years later, unnoticed in the general excitement of America's entry into the First World War.

THE GREAT WAR called for the participation of a number of artists, such as James Montgomery Flagg, who created posters for recruitment drives, and Abbott H. Thayer, whose book *Concealing Coloration in the Animal Kingdom* was the basis for military camouflage techniques. The Ten proceeded serenely through the upheavals of these years, their art inexorably drifting toward bland decorativeness. Hassam, alone of the group, was stimulated by and reacted with great vigor to the fact of the war. Between 1916 and 1919, he was absorbed in the creation of a sequence of paintings known as the *Flag Series*. These pictures are the ultimate development of his Impressionist style. Moreover, there is a note of modernism that cautiously infuses some of the *Flag Series* pictures, as may be seen in the flat patterning of the massed flags. Hassam was not unaware of the changes that had overtaken art in the new century. Some of this restlessness originated within factions of the New York art world even as the Ten were first making public their own mild form of dissent. At the turn of the century Robert Henri had led a generally younger and more progressive group of artists, the Eight, in a search for values that would be more closely related to the realities of modern urban life. As John Sloan put it,

> ...[W]e were opposed to impressionism, with its blue shadows and orange lights because it seemed "unreal." We chose our colors from observation of facts and qualities of the *things* we painted, with little reference to phenomena of light effects. ... We realists. ... were revolting against the corruption of eyesight painting. ...

Even so, the two groups had much in common; both Sloan and Henri painted landscapes in a style that has been described by art historian John Baur as "dark impressionism." Hassam's group and that of Henri show two aspects of that concern for realism that had provided continuity in American art in the 19th century. But what suddenly preempted the more orthodox Impressionism of the Ten, as well as the "dark" movement of the Eight, with its social-realist orientation, was the formal revolution of the modernists. For the first time since emerging from a Colonial culture, American art was faced with a distinctly novel and challenging concept that resisted accommodation within the luminist-realist tradition.

The occasion for the commencement of this revolution was the Armory Show, or more properly, the International Exhibition of Modern Art, which opened at New York's 69th Regiment Armory on February 13, 1913. This exhibition introduced European post-Impressionism and Cubism in depth to the American public for the first time. Of the some 1,300 works of art included, one-third were foreign, the rest were by American artists. Of the Ten, only Hassam, Twachtman (posthumously), and Weir were invited to participate by the show's sponsor, the Association of American Painters and Sculptors, whose criteria for selection paid special attention to "distinct individuality of expression and forceful manifestation of creative power," and who requested the artists chosen to "expose works in which the personal note is distinctly sounded."[3] Hassam responded by sending six oils, five pastels, and a drawing. One painting, *Vesuvius* (Collection Joseph H. Hirshhorn, New York), a work from his third European trip, was deemed important enough to be reproduced as one of the fifty-seven halftone postcards of objects in the exhibition, which the Association issued as part of its overall program of public education. Much has been written about the effects of this remarkable event on the history of American art. The modern consensus is that the Armory Show served to exert a "profound effect on artists, collectors, and the art market [and] transformed the character of American art."[4] Hassam, however, remained skeptical of what he saw at the Armory Show, feeling that much of it was fraudulent, an attempt merely to shock. But he was confident that "if any of it is good, it will stay on the Golden Bough of Art. So much of it is obviously insincere and on the fool-fringe of the Fine Arts that it will rot and drop off."

By 1915, Hassam was showing a keen interest in printmaking, especially etching, probably in response to the general reawakening of interest in graphics in the United States. (Indeed, art historian Carl Zigrosser sees 1915 as the year the etching process began to revive after its hiatus after the death of Whistler.) That summer Hassam and his wife had gone to Cos Cob, a village near Greenwich, Connecticut, where he had access to an etching press owned by a friend, making it "easier to work and get proofs quickly." By November 1915, when he was given an exhibition in New York at the galleries of Frederick Keppel and Co., Hassam had completed seventy-five etchings and drypoints, including four plates that he had started in 1887 and 1898 but had never completed. This was a prodigy of work, considering the brief time involved. There is a great diversity of subject matter in this first group of etchings: landscapes, seascapes, and portraits, including one of Maude. A seascape entitled *Old Lace* because of its subject, surf foam, was acknowledged in the exhibition catalogue as "one of the most delicately bitten plates, technically, in the etched work of the world." Adeline Adams observed of Hassam that "with a mind enriched by thirty years of sedulous communion with Nature. ... he re-created in the black-and-white of his proofs the illusions of that quivering radiance of light and color which had so often ... suffused his canvas." Joseph Pennell, Whistler's biographer and a superb graphic artist in his own right, was duly impressed by Hassam's sudden and complete command of etching technique. As the years passed, Hassam continued to devote much time to etching; in 1925, he was honored by the appearance of a book on this aspect of his career, published by Charles Scribner's Sons, New York. A special edition of 350 copies was also prepared, containing an original etching as the frontispiece of each. By 1933, when the Leonard Clayton Gallery published a catalogue raisonné of Hassam's etchings and drypoints, 376 copper plates were identified, the results of eighteen years of work.

Lithography attracted Hassam's interest about 1917. That medium was experiencing a considerable revival following the publication of Joseph Pennell's lithographs of the construction of the Panama Canal in a book called *The Wonder of Work*. Hassam's lithographs avoided the usual method of drawing with wax crayon on the stone; instead, he used the fluid tusche like watercolor, applying it with a brush. The resulting prints were highly acclaimed for both their spontaneity and richness of tone. He was very proud

---

[3] Milton W. Brown, *The Story of the Armory Show* (New York: New York Graphic Society, 1963), p. 65.
[4] Brown, p. 212

FIFTH AVENUE, NOON, 1916. *Etching. The Metropolitan Museum of Art (Gift of Mrs. Childe Hassam, 1940).*

reer, a tacit admission that his allegiance was to an older, more secure order of life and art which was passing swiftly into history. Certainly, he had won enough recognition. Almost every other year since capturing a bronze medal at the Paris Exposition Universelle of 1889, he had received medals for his paintings at the major American exhibitions—the Carnegie International, Pittsburgh; the Corcoran Biennial, Washington, D.C.: and the Pennsylvania Academy Annual, Philadelphia. His paintings had been collected by some of the principal patrons of American art, including George A. Hearn, John Gellatly, and Charles Freer. By 1935, the Metropolitan Museum of Art in New York had purchased five of his canvases, as many as the museum had of Weir's and Twachtman's paintings combined. He had been prominent in the major art exhibition of the decade in the West, which had been sponsored in 1915, by the great San Francisco Panama-Pacific Exposition, and his work had been exhibited also in Denver and Los Angeles. But these accomplishments could not outweigh the fact that traditional values in art were yielding to the "formal revolution of the modernists."

Changing, too, was the way artists were brought to the public's attention. The old system of artists' societies and institutional support, such as the National Academy, was being replaced by dealers who acted as artists' representatives. William Macbeth, Charles Daniel, Alfred Stieglitz, and N. E. Montross became prominent in the first decades of the new century for their enthusiastic support of new forms of artistic expression. All along Fifth Avenue, from 34th Street, where M. Knoedler's gallery stood, north to 57th Street, dealers were opening storefront galleries, where modern art, both foreign and American, could be seen in profusion. When Hassam's dealer of nine years' standing, Montross, opened his gallery to the modernists in 1914, the association between them cooled noticeably. By 1919, Hassam was exhibiting at the more conservative Milch Gallery, which became the principal dealer for his paintings.

AS THE MODERNISTS assumed command on Fifth Avenue, Hassam retreated to a private world which was proof against the barbarisms that he saw being committed in the name of art. In an interview granted to De Witt Lockman, in 1927, Hassam acknowledged that he had come to appreciate certain ideas derived from classicism, and that he owed this to Kenyon Cox. Although Cox was an archfoe of Impressionism, neither could he tolerate modern art, and, in 1911, he published in book form a series of lectures he had delivered on the classic view of art. The effect on Hassam's landscape painting was a shift away from a legitimate dialogue with color and form toward an extraneous and often distracting substantive element. By injecting "classical" figures into the compositions of his landscapes, Hassam frequently disturbed the esthetic integrity of his pictures. Reviewing his 1915 exhibition at the Montross Gallery, the critic Charles L. Buchanan observed,

> If a sheer facility be (as some think) a cardinal virtue, then Mr. Hassam stands, beyond the shadow of a doubt, at the head of American painting. In his characteristic way, he is incomparable. But . . . his taste is not always unimpeachable. He will put as exquisite a bit of painting on canvas as

of these accomplishments—as with his mastery of painting almost a half century earlier, it had been mostly self-education and confidence that had guided him from novice to master in his profession. His life had been orderly, and nearing the end of it, Hassam sensed a kind of symmetry: "I began my career in the graphic arts, and I am ending it in the graphic arts."

Of course, that was an overstatement; Hassam continued to paint well into the early 1930's. Yet, it is significant that his final one-man exhibition of paintings was in spring 1929 at the Macbeth Gallery in New York, and that the retrospective exhibition organized by the Albright Art Gallery in Buffalo the same year was the last survey of his painting career mounted in the artist's lifetime. Thereafter, until his death in 1935, it was Hassam's etchings and lithographs which exclusively interested the dealers and museums. So far as the public was concerned, Hassam the painter had ceased to exist. There is a certain ruefulness in Hassam's remark about the ending of his ca-you could wish and irretrievably ruin it by the incongruous intrusion of some stupid, superfluous, crudely indicated nude.

Like most Impressionists, Hassam's forte was not figure painting, but in his *New York Window* series one usually finds a harmonious adjustment between the figure and the interior space that surrounds it. And when he chose to paint a portrait—he never painted men—one is conscious that, first and foremost, his goal was not primarily a likeness of the sitter, but the creation of an evocative mood through color. The more idealized portraits still tended to relate to notions of classicism, especially when the sitter was presented in profile and the coiffure was gathered at the back of the head.

If, in fact, Hassam had been searching for the ideal landscape, as his travels of thirty summers suggest, he found it at last on the eastern end of Long Island. William Merritt Chase made the town of Shinnecock famous when he established a summer art colony there in 1891, and, over the years, artists began frequenting the villages between Southampton and Montauk. Hassam visited East Hampton as early as 1909, but it was not until the summer of 1917 that the place finally claimed him. East Hampton combined the isolation of Appledore and the Colonial charm of Old Lyme. In 1920, Hassam and his wife acquired a rambling frame house on Egypt Lane, which they made a permanent summer address. The great elms bordering the main street, the weathered, clapboard houses, and the gently rolling hills of the countryside came to be recurring themes in his summers' work. In time, East Hampton's motifs became as identified with his art as were those of Appledore or Old Lyme. The long, empty white beaches that stretched east and west into the shimmering hazy light have neither the elemental starkness of Appledore, nor the gentleness of Old Lyme, but, as at those places, the quality of light at East Hampton is modified by its proximity to the ocean. Hassam found this quality essential to his art, and he created some of his most chromatically brilliant work during his East Hampton years. The size of his pictures became correspondingly large, as if to embrace the whole of nature, and he began to employ a broader, freer brush stroke. There is an exuberance about these Long Island landscapes that speaks of a youthful spirit, in spite of the fact that the artist was approaching his seventieth year.

As the idyllic summers at East Hampton crowded upon one another, Hassam gradually exalted what had, at first, been only a marginal interest in classicism into a major preoccupation. A review of his one-man exhibition in a January 1925 *Time* magazine seemed to question Hassam's judgement, if not his mental competence:

> Gods live in [Montauk], so says the brush of Mr. Hassam. *Diana as Spring* bursts arrowy-footed through the wood.... [In] *The Grove of Aphrodite,* nymphs move to pipes unseen ... *Dryads* dance upon a blowy hill.... It is not strange then that one of Mr. Hassam's canvasses [sic] should depict no less a scene than *Adam and Eve Walking out in Montauk in the Early Spring.*

But advancing age and innate conservatism led him to retrench stubbornly, heeding only his own convictions as he had always

EASTHAMPTON, 1917. *Etching. The Metropolitan Museum of Art (Gift of Mrs. Childe Hassam, 1940).*

done. He would not be deterred by criticism of this sort, and he still had a loyal following among conservative museum directors and collectors across the nation. Frank Jewett Mather, Jr., in his catalogue introduction to Hassam's 1926 exhibition at Durand-Ruel Galleries, declared that "Childe Hassam's pictures seem sufficiently at home on walls where we are accustomed to seeing Monet, Pissarro, and Sisley." And Hassam's champion in Los Angeles, the collector William Preston Harrison, advised the director of the Los Angeles County Museum that, "I believe it is now generally conceded that outside of John S. Sargent, Childe Hassam is the biggest figure in [the] American art world. He is criticised, roasted and knocked, but never belittled by his enemies."

TO THE CONSERVATIVE art establishment, Hassam was the grand old man of American art. Honors came to him, but he did not bask in celebrity. In 1920, his old friend Gari Melchers proposed him for election to the American Academy of Arts and Letters. (The nomination was seconded by a group of distinguished colleagues that included the sculptor Daniel Chester French.) The same year, Louis Comfort Tiffany persuaded Hassam to serve on the art advisory committee of the Tiffany Foundation; Hassam consented on the condition that he be allowed to criticize the classes of the Foundation's Art Guild school at Oyster Bay. Summoned to purely ceremonial functions at the American Academy, he frequently replied with testy observations about the dubious worth of such things. These he scrawled on the invitation cards and summarily returned to the Academy—such nonsense meant time away from work.

Hassam's schedule was absolutely regular by the late 1920's and early 1930's. At the beginning of every summer, he and Maude departed for East Hampton, returning to New York each fall to prepare for the round of exhibitions sponsored by the major eastern art institutions. Invariably, he sent one or two paintings to the National

LAFAYETTE STREET, 1918. *Lithograph and lithotint. The Metropolitan Museum of Art (Gift of Mrs. Childe Hassam, 1940).*

Academy of Design; he always expected to win a prize, but, by this time, it rarely happened. If prizes came in those years, they were for his etchings. In 1931, the Pennsylvania Academy awarded him a gold medal for etching in memory of Joseph Pennell. Many of his old friends of the Ten were gone now; De Camp, Weir, Twachtman, and Reid had died, and then Simmons, in 1931. Since about 1907, he and Maude had occupied a studio apartment at 130 West 57th Street. Now his life offered mostly the satisfaction of having labored honestly at making art a joyous testament to life and the world of color. Each spring brought the prospect of another glorious summer at East Hampton, and this undoubtedly revived his spirits. His last active summer there melted into autumn. He and Maude stayed on through the middle of October, as they had done for so many years, but the local East Hampton *Star* found this occasion merited particular notice:

> Childe Hassam spent his 75th birthday in East Hampton yesterday with the usual quiet celebration of the event at his home on Egypt Lane . . . with a walk [and] a drive to view the autumn foliage . . . Mr. Hassam is one of the latest bathers here and did enjoy a swim up to the last cold snap a week ago.

That winter in New York, Hassam fell ill. He did little work that season; recuperation was depressingly slow, and he probably looked forward to being cured that summer at his cherished East Hampton. When spring arrived, he was still an invalid, and had to be taken out to East Hampton in an ambulance. The summer passed without recovery, and, finally, at the end of August 1935, he died.

In a somewhat belated recognition of Hassam's achievements, the National Academy finally awarded him its coveted Saltus Medal for Merit in 1935. It had been nine years since the Academy had honored him with a prize. But in his last days, Hassam's thoughts were not fixed on such transient matters. He had been thinking ahead to the time when young artists would be coming along who needed help. To this end, he established "The Hassam Fund," named in Maude's honor, not his own. The Fund would be activated after his death through the periodic sale of the works he bequeathed to the American Academy of Arts and Letters. This act was typical of Hassam's magnanimity of spirit, and it was his final and most profound expression of faith in the future of American art. The roots of Western culture lay deep in the richness of a common tradition, and the "Golden Bough of Art," as he characterized it, would continue to bear fruit cultivated as much by the European past as it was by the American present. The American Academy honored Hassam's memory and his legacy at a convocation on November 12, 1936. The text of the tribute was written by the dean of American art critics, Royall Cortissoz, and read by the music director and conductor of the New York Philharmonic Orchestra, Dr. Walter Damrosch. It might have embarrassed Hassam to hear that, "he had the American way of profiting by European example without falling victim to European convention," but he probably would have concurred with that summation. That is what he had striven to do, and that is what he would have advised the new generation of artists to attempt.

PLATE 1

RAINY DAY, BOSTON
1885
Oil on canvas
26¼" x 48¼" (66.6 cm x 122.5 cm)
The Toledo Museum of Art, Toledo,
Ohio
(Gift of Florence Scott Libbey)

Hassam returned from his first European trip in the fall of 1883, and began to employ oil paint, rather than watercolor, as his primary medium. His abiding interest in Turner's view of the world, with its emphasis upon the drama of atmospheric effects, may have exerted some influence upon Hassam's treatment of thematic material, but he was responding primarily as a realist painter to the stimuli of life around him. As Hassam recalled, "In Boston, among [my] earliest subjects were the city streets . . . scenes with wet pavements, which they say I invented. Nobody had ever done that before. [The reflections on] the asphalt appealed to me." Of course, the French Impressionists had painted such scenes a decade earlier, but it is unlikely that as early as 1885 Hassam had come into contact with such paintings as Claude Monet's *Le Pont Neuf, Paris* (1872), which takes a nearly identical approach to a city view as does *Rainy Day, Boston.* This painting, therefore, must be regarded as a synthesis of the influences, other than French Impressionism, that were available to him at this time—the Barbizon School and tonalism.

The result is a work that avoids the excesses of late 19th-century sentimental genre by subordinating the genre elements to a dominant interest in the poetry of mood. Here Hassam also invents a composition of unusual complexity. The format he has chosen, nearly a double square, suggests two separate works, an idea that is reinforced by the two diverging vistas. Unification is achieved by the dramatic diagonal that extends from the upper left, following the perspective line of the rooftops, to the lower right, where it is anchored by the detail of the tether ring at the curb and the artist's signature. Triangles dominate the compositional scheme, both at the level of the picture plane, and as the element responsible for the illusion of deep space. The convincing aerial perspective, with its palpable, mist-laden pearly light, reinforces the drawing to produce a painting of striking realism. This realism is achieved with a great economy of means, both in terms of color and brushwork—one is not at first glance particularly conscious of either. Rather, it is the presentation of an integrated spacial unity that makes this picture so convincing.

The view represented in *Rainy Day, Boston* is the double prospect of Columbus Avenue to the left looking east to the Public Gardens, and Appleton Street giving off to the southeast. After their marriage in February 1884, the Hassams took up residence at 282 Columbus Avenue, in the section of Boston known as the South End. Hassam's studio was on Tremont Street; to get there he traveled the length of Columbus Avenue, probably by the same horse-drawn streetcar seen in the middle distance in the painting. This scene, therefore, was thoroughly familiar to him, and represents not so much a particular view, as a distillation of the artist's responses to the emotions evoked by certain qualities of light and atmosphere.

23

PLATE 2

BOSTON COMMON AT
TWILIGHT
1885–86
Oil on canvas
42″ x 60″ (106.7 cm x 152.4 cm)
Museum of Fine Arts, Boston
(Gift of Maude E. Appleton)

Although Hassam never referred to James A. M. Whistler as an influence on his work, *Boston Common at Twilight* reveals qualities that surely point to this possibility. In 1883, the year Hassam first visited London, Whistler had held a large exhibition of his work at the Fine Arts Society. His experiments with painting the effects of evening light, the famous "nocturnes," had already made him a prominent, if sometimes controversial, figure in the London art world. It is most likely that Hassam knew of Whistler's achievements as an etcher and lithographer, since the bulk of the latter's graphic art was produced between 1871 and 1880. But most importantly, Whistler represented a continuation of a tradition in the painting of nature that began with Turner. Moreover, he was working in the then most innovative non-French style of tonalism. Like Impressionism, tonalism eschewed all purely descriptive or literary references; and Whistler, as Wanda Corn has pointed out, was "instrumental in tonalism's being the mainstream esthetic [in American art] that it was in the 1880s and 1890s." Certainly, Hassam's Boston Common subject resorts to the kind of flat "arrangement" of objects so typical of Whistler's style. And Hassam's conceit of the crescent moon emblem, which he added to his signature at this time in reference to the Near Eastern flavor of his name after he dropped the use of "Frederick," is too reminiscent of Whistler's famous butterfly device to be coincidental.

Hassam's paintings tended to become progressively larger during the 1880's, as he worked toward achieving greater expressive power. The Boston Common subject is twice as large as *Rainy Day, Boston* (Plate 1) of the previous year, yet it is a more compactly organized work in terms of design. This preoccupation with size culminated in 1889 with a painting entitled *Autumn*, now lost, that measured ten feet in length. Physical size could draw attention to an artist's work, especially in the context of a group show. However, it also presented a practical problem for potential clients, as Philip Hendy, the former owner of *Boston Common at Twilight*, noted: "My father had it hanging in his office a good many years before he had a house large enough to accommodate it." This tendency also implies a need on the part of the artist to involve the spectator physically by extending the boundaries of the painting nearly to the limits of peripheral vision. After all, the primary aim of Tonalism was to envelop the eye of the beholder in the poetry of nature's moods.

Shortly after his return from Europe in the fall of 1883, Hassam leased a studio at 149 Tremont Street. The building had a favorable location, since it faced north, and the Common opposite provided an unobstructed source of light. The view Hassam chose for this work looks south on Tremont Street toward the intersection of Boylston Street, just across from his studio. *Boston Common at Twilight* possesses a breadth of vision and the kind of profound sincerity in rendering scenes of ordinary life that prompted Philip Hendy to call it "a very genuine picture of life rendered by honest and simple means."

PLATE 3

UNE AVERSE, RUE BONAPARTE
1887
Oil on canvas
40¼" x 77¼" (102.2 cm x 196.2 cm)
Private Collection, Wichita, Kansas

Hassam's move to Paris in 1886 did not bring about any immediate change in the concept of his art. His first paintings done there were variations on the theme of the urban landscape which he had been developing in Boston. These new Paris scenes showed his continuing interest in the uses of dramatic perspective, well-recognized subject matter, and moody atmospheric effects achieved via a grayed palette. While some familiar elements seem to be carried over directly from *Rainy Day, Boston* (Plate 1), especially the treatment of the wet pavement, *Une Averse, Rue Bonaparte* shows a progression toward a more subtle use of color, as well as a freer drawing and brushwork, that proclaims a steady growth of ability.

It is Hassam's deliberate avoidance of the picturesque that one finds consistent in his work. Rather than paint the celebrated landmarks of Paris, Hassam sought out the ordinary scenes of city life. This prospect of the Rue Bonaparte ignores the more colorful Place St. Sulpice, with its magnificent 17th-century church and the renowned Medici Fountain, although it is just to the left of the view he has chosen to paint. Instead, he concentrated his attention on the Luxembourg Gardens, indicated by the small mansarded house at the end of the street in the distance. The subject of this painting is really the poignant bleakness of the street, dominated by the poster-covered wall surrounding the old seminary of St. Sulpice, the somber line of waiting horse-drawn cabs, and the humble condition of the ordinary passersby, caught in a sudden shower.

Hassam cited this painting as his first Paris subject, and, since he dated it 1887, it must have been the product of many months' work. The following year, when he exhibited *Une Averse* at the Salon, it was greatly praised and became something of a sensation. Certainly, this was not the most innovative kind of painting to be seen in Paris during these years. Henri Rousseau, the inspired primitive, had shown his strange, dream-like pictures for the first time at the Salon des Indépendents in 1886; and the leader of French Impressionism, Claude Monet, had expressed a desire to paint without any substantive references to nature whatsoever. Yet, for all of his conservatism, Hassam's youthful achievement formed an effective bridge between more conventional forms of realist painting and Impressionism.

PLATE 4

LE JOUR DU GRAND PRIX
1887
Oil on canvas
36" x 48" (91.4 cm x 122 cm)
The New Britain Museum of American Art, New Britain, Connecticut

The year 1887 marked Hassam's passage from the modified tonalist manner, in which he had been working since 1885, to a full commitment to the blond palette of Impressionism. He did not hesitate to revert occasionally to tonalist mood, however, especially when a particular subject required this approach to pictorial problems. The 1888 *April Showers, Champs Elysées* (Joslyn Art Museum, Omaha) is a case in point. Yet the Paris pictures display a more assured brushwork than before—the technique is suave, with a buttery impasto not present in the Boston scenes. In another quite different painting, *La Crépuscule* (Hammer Galleries, New York), done in the same year, Hassam continued his interest in the effects of diminished light noted in such works as *Boston Common at Twilight* (Plate 2). The difference now is that in the Paris subject his command of muted color harmonies has been altered through a greater awareness of the Impressionist idiom. This wavering between the styles of tonalism and Impressionism in the period 1887–88 offers an insight into Hassam's search for the resolution of pictorial problems and his striving for a mature, personal style of painting.

Le Jour du Grand Prix was Hassam's first essay into Impressionism, but it was not the product of the free and spontaneous *plein air* methods normally associated with the style. Before attempting this work, he made a smaller, nearly identical version, *Grand Prix Day*, (1887; Museum of Fine Arts, Boston), in which all of the problems of composition and color were rehearsed. *Le Jour du Grand Prix* was a painting destined for exhibition at the Salon of 1888, and it may be assumed that Hassam wished to achieve the assured performance possible only through rigorous preparation. Portions of the final version more deliberately approximate the staccato brushstrokes of Impressionism, notably in the sky and foreground areas, which are treated in a far less agitated way in the preparatory work.

The choice of Impressionist method, the bright colors, and the dramatic range of values in the Grand Prix painting seem to have evolved naturally as a response to the character of the subject, rather than as a self-conscious experiment. The occasion it celebrated was one of the most festive moments in the Paris social season. Here on the Avenue de l'Impératrice, as it was known in the 19th century, the *beau monde* in their elegant carriages promenaded between the Arc de Triomphe and the race course known as the Hippodrome de Longchamp in the Bois de Boulogne for the annual running of the Grand Prix. Hassam captured the spirit of La Belle Epoque as few artists ever have, and registered it in this painting with all the éclat of a brass band. His efforts met with notable success: the painting won a gold medal in the Salon of 1888.

PLATE 5

AU GRAND PRIX DE PARIS
1887
Pastel on paper
18" x 12" (45.7 cm x 30.4 cm)
The Corcoran Gallery of Art, Washington, D.C.

Beginning in the 18th century, pastel had been associated historically with French art. Later, the Barbizon painters, especially Jean François Millet, used it extensively. Hassam surely saw examples of Millet's pastels in the collection brought to Boston by William Morris Hunt, who is known to have practiced pastel painting himself. This medium of colored chalks is ideally suited to rapid sketching out of doors. Pastel colors are generally high-keyed in hue and soft in texture. Both properties enhance the atmospheric rendering of nature sought by the Impressionists. Thus it was logical that the pastel medium emerged as a serious vehicle for artistic expression in Paris, in 1874, when Degas, Morisot, Monet, and Renoir showed pastel paintings in the first Impressionist exhibition. Mary Cassatt, the only American in the group, who participated in the fourth Impressionist exhibition in 1879, was a friend and admirer of Degas. Her work was greatly influenced by him, especially in the use of pastels. Whistler was also working with the medium in Venice at this time. So, by the early 1880's, the principal figures of the Impressionist movement, both French and American, were fostering a major revival of pastel. Not surprisingly, a number of young New Yorkers—among them, Robert Blum, Edwin Blashfield,

and Carroll Beckwith—formed the Society of American Painters in Pastel on their return from studies in Paris. In the same year, 1882, there appeared, in the widely read American periodical *The Art Amateur*, the first of a series of articles on pastel painting. Two years later, when the Society held its first exhibition in New York, much attention was given to the publication event.[5]

It is uncertain whether Hassam experimented with pastel before his three-year residence in Paris. Very likely, he did not take it up seriously before 1886, but when he did, Hassam immediately assumed a commanding grasp of the technique. Perhaps not coincidentally, his best examples are scenes of the race track, a subject that Degas had made his own. For Hassam, the subject of fashionable spectators in the boxes at Longchamp exerted a strong appeal—he loved the assemblage of colorful costumes and the character of the *boulevardiers* and their elegant ladies, and drew them, as one reviewer observed, with "a gusto [that] convinces his public in every crayon stroke that it is a fine thing to be a painter." Hassam joined the Society of American Painters in Pastel in 1890, following his return to America. His work was included in the Society's fourth and last exhibition that year, and received praiseworthy attention.

[5] For a discussion of the development of pastel painting in America, and history of the Society of American Painters in Pastel, see Theodore E. Stebbins, Jr., *American Master Drawings and Watercolors* (New York: Harper & Row, 1976), pp. 224-233.

PLATE 6

MRS. HASSAM IN THEIR GARDEN
1889
Oil on canvas
34" x 52½" (86.4 cm x 134.3 cm)
Collection Mrs. Norman Woolworth, New York

In the paintings of his early maturity, Hassam's personality is often submerged within his subject matter. This often reveals a strong element of romanticism lurking beneath the brilliant surface manipulations of paint. The tendency emerges most strongly in a number of extraordinarily intimate pictures painted between 1888 and 1894, all of which establish a deliberate romantic parallel between women and flowers. It is a theme Hassam would return to much later with his figure studies of women in interiors, but this garden picture, and other variations of it, such as *The Flower Garden* (1888; Worcester Art Museum) and *A Sunny Morning, Villiers-le-Bel* (1888; formerly Collection of Mr. and Mrs. Albert E. Lehman), stand as Hassam's most intensely felt statements about the female "mystique."

During their residence in Paris, the Hassams formed a close friendship with a French family who lived in the town of Villiers-le-Bel, some ten miles outside the city. Occasional visits were Hassam's only excursions into the French countryside, so the pictures painted at Villiers-le-Bel partake more of the Impressionist penchant for nature than the bulk of his *oeuvre* during these years. Here Hassam explored the effects of dappled sunlight and cool shadow in works very reminiscent of the paintings of Frédéric Bazille and Claude Monet of twenty years earlier. Yet, for Hassam, these garden scenes were advances into a more brilliant colorism than he had thus far dared. There is also a note of modernity in the composition that emancipates these pictures from being merely derivative of the older work of the French Impressionists. *Mrs. Hassam in Their Garden* is an ingratiating mixture of flat and agitated brushwork, through which the artist attempts to fuse descriptive realism with Impressionist color and mood. Modern also is the use of interlocking pattern and the flattening of pictorial space through the emphasis upon horizontal and vertical bands of color. There are strong echoes of Whistler's "arrangements"; however, one is always struck by Hassam's own pictorial acuity—his ability to state succinctly the essence of his subject. He presents his subject in a natural and plausible way, yet Hassam's pictures are always infused by a thoroughly artistic sensibility.

PLATE 7

WASHINGTON ARCH IN SPRING
1890
Oil on canvas
26" x 21½" (66 cm x 55 cm)
The Phillips Collection, Washington, D.C.

The Hassams returned to America in the fall of 1889, and took up residence at 95 Fifth Avenue, New York. During their years abroad, New York had continued its prodigious construction of public and private buildings of the greatest magnificence. Fifth Avenue was the focus of this activity:

> In the era following the Civil War an army of new millionaires moving to Fifth Avenue brought wealth to the city. And, like Collis P. Huntington and Darius Ogden Mills, they continued to bring it until well after the turn of the century. They brought it from the copper mines of Montana and the gold mines of California, from the silver lodes of Nevada, from the slaughterhouses of Chicago and the forests of Michigan, and from all the great railroads that were opening up the West. To these new rich, a house on Fifth Avenue was the crowning symbol of success.[6]

New York, in many respects, was beginning to rival Paris as a cultural capital. The Metropolitan Museum of Art had opened, and the decade of the 1880's saw the construction of the Metropolitan Opera House. Two of the city's permanent symbols of cultural pride, the Brooklyn Bridge and the Statue of Liberty, also came into existence in that decade.

The south end of Fifth Avenue, where Hassam had his studio in 1890, was "old New York," the New York of Henry James's *Washington Square*, and that of Edith Wharton's *Age of Innocence*. At the foot of this splendid avenue stood a wooden arch, designed by one of America's most prestigious architects, Stanford White, to commemorate the 100th anniversary of George Washington's inauguration. Painted to simulate stone (it was replaced a few years later in actual stone), the arch undoubtedly reminded Hassam of its famous ancestor in Paris. The artist's Impressionist treatment of the subject completes the allusion—this thoroughly American scene has been painted in the best French manner. A sense of light and air permeates this picture, which is dominated by the feathery branches of the elm trees, through which the arch seems to glow with morning light. At the same time, Hassam does not fail to observe the actualities of the life of the street; the street sweeper, the nurse with perambulator, the elegant coach and driver waiting by the curb. Yet these human elements are not particularized as they were in *Rainy Day Boston* (Plate 1) or *Une Averse, Rue Bonaparte* (Plate 3). Rather, they now assume a more organic function within the total composition.

[6] S.C. Burchell, "On the Avenue, Fifth Avenue," *New York, N.Y.* (New York, 1968), p. 19.

PLATE 8

**CRYSTAL PALACE,
CHICAGO EXPOSITION**
1893
Oil on canvas
18" x 26" (45.7 cm x 66 cm)
Collection Mrs. Norman Woolworth,
New York

The World's Columbian Exposition, honoring the 400th anniversary of the discovery of America, opened on May 1, 1893. The site for this event was Jackson Park, 685 acres just outside the city of Chicago on Lake Michigan. Nearly three times the size of the Centennial Exposition held in Philadelphia in 1876, the Columbian Exposition was the product of the combined talents of America's greatest architects, painters, and sculptors. The declaration by the President of the United States at the opening ceremonies that this Exposition would influence the dignity, welfare, and freedom of all mankind was symbolic of the mood of euphoria of the more than 27 million people who attended the year-long celebration. The sculptor Augustus St. Gaudens firmly believed that the Exposition represented the greatest assembly of artists since the 15th century.

The White City, as the exposition complex was called, was but the latest manifestation of an international fervor for large-scale exhibitions of the world's arts and manufacturers. The chief planners of the White City, Daniel Burnham and John Root, assembled the most distinguished architects of the nation, including Richard Morris Hunt and McKim, Mead & White, who provided the designs for a spectacular "city of palaces." The Beaux-Arts style of building they favored instantly set the standard of excellence for architecture nationwide.

Like all large expositions of the time, the White City included a Department of Fine Arts, which was devoted to the exhibition of paintings and sculpture. The Paris Exposition Universelle of 1889 had set the precedent of awarding prizes to participating artists, and generally had fostered the concept of art as an integral part of international commerce. In Chicago, hundreds of artists took part, not only submitting paintings and sculpture for display in the Fine Arts pavilion itself, but also providing mural decorations for the colossal buildings and temporary sculptures on the exposition site. Hassam made "some wash drawings of [architectural] elevations ... putting in people and skies" which were used as visualizations for the proposed project. He was also represented in the Fine Arts Department exhibition by six oil paintings and four watercolors, and came away with a bronze medal.

While visiting Chicago that summer of 1893, Hassam painted a few scenes of the Exposition. Like all artists attempting to capture the overpowering monumentality of the White City, Hassam could only allude to the scale upon which it was built. In this glimpse of the dome of the Crystal Palace, he managed to suggest that scale, though this exercise really concerns the solution of pictorial problems of space and color, not documentation. Here he employed a broader, freer brushstroke to convey a sense of immediacy—the picture seems to have been created as a direct and spontaneous response to the excitement of brilliant sunlight.

PLATE 9

THE ROOM OF FLOWERS
1894

Oil on canvas
34" x 34" (86.4 cm x 86.4 cm)
Collection Mr. and Mrs. Arthur G.
Altschul, New York

During the summer of 1890, Hassam renewed his acquaintance with Celia Laighton Thaxter, who had been one of his pupils in the watercolor classes he conducted in Boston in the early 1880's. Even before then, Mrs. Thaxter had gained a measure of recognition for her book *Among the Isles of Shoals*, a description of life along her native New Hampshire coast, published in 1873, as well as for a volume of poetry *Drift-Wood*, which appeared six years later.

Since 1848, the Laighton family had operated a summer resort hotel on the island of Appledore, one of the Isles of Shoals some ten miles off the Maine-New Hampshire coast. Appledore House was the scene of annual summer gatherings of artists and literati from New England and New York. Hassam's old friends, the painters Ross Turner and Ignaz Gaugengigl were frequent visitors, and it was there that Hassam also met Richard Watson Gilder, poet and editor of *Century* magazine. That first summer at Appledore made a strong impression upon Hassam. He and Maude would return periodically over the next decade, and there he painted some of his most powerful landscapes.

The deep affection that grew between Hassam and the older Celia Thaxter is evident in the many sonnets she composed in his honor. The earliest, dated July 25, 1890, is a play upon the crescent moon device he used at the time to sign his painting. It begins,

A crescent with its glory just begun,
A spark from the great central fires sublime,
A crescent that shall orb into a sun,
And burn resplendent through the mists of time.

Celia Thaxter was then writing another collection of poems, to be published under the title *An Island Garden*, and had asked Hassam to provide illustrations for it. Perhaps in return for this compliment, Hassam painted this view of the Thaxter drawing room at Appledore, which had been the scene of so many festive gatherings. An agglomeration of objects in the late Victorian taste, the room was "filled with flowers and most everything else, from a Grand Rapids rocking chair to the most exquisite Venetian glass and period pieces of colonial furniture. . . ." The artist has included his friend in the painting in such a casual way as to very nearly lose her in the picture's complicated design.

The Room of Flowers is an early example of Hassam's use of the square format, which was then becoming a popular canvas shape in the work of the American Impressionists, notably Twachtman and Willard Metcalf. The square is a static shape that creates no visual movement of its own. Instead, it emphasizes the internal formal relationships of a painting in a way that heightens the purely abstract function of color, line, and mass. Accordingly, this painting is conceived almost entirely in a very narrow value scale of bright colors, which emphasize surface pattern. In that sense, the picture comes closer to the spirit of expressionism than to Impressionism. Yet Hassam does not quite reach such a high threshold. *The Room of Flowers* is, after all, permeated by a kind of sentimental poetry in its conceit of Celia Thaxter as one of the room's flowers.

PLATE 10

PLACE CENTRALE AND FORT CABANAS, HAVANA
1895
Oil on canvas
21¼" x 26¼" (54 cm x 66.6 cm)
The Detroit Institute of Arts, Detroit, Michigan

Early in 1895, Hassam made his first and only trip to the Caribbean. The circumstances surrounding this unusual departure from his routine are not clear. In the company of Frank Robinson, a coal merchant who sold coal in Cuba, he traveled to Havana and worked there for over a month. He visited some sugar plantations near the capital and painted palm trees, but his most ambitious work was this view of the city, taken from his hotel window on the Place Centrale. In his 1927 interview with De Witt Lockman, Hassam recalled that the sight of the Spanish flag flying over Fort Cabanas seemed especially significant historically. Indeed, even as he was working on this painting, Cuban revolutionary forces were beginning their efforts to overthrow Spanish rule: "We left Havana on the last day before the Cuban insurrection started [February 24, 1895]. It was the last time that the Spanish flag flew in the Western Hemisphere."

Hassam chose to paint the scene in the broad light of noonday, with the sun casting shadows directly away from his viewpoint. The effect is to flatten the landscape into bands of alternating dark and light colors. Distance is created mainly by aerial perspective, through the progressive graying of hues from the picture's foreground to the horizon. This rather calculated avoidance of linear perspective, formerly so central to Hassam's pictorial space, and his sole dependence upon color to achieve depth, mark the beginning of a new phase in his art. Its importance was acknowledged by the jury of the National Academy of Design's annual exhibition of 1895, who awarded the painting the Webb Prize. We know Hassam held a special regard for this work. He considered it one of his "best things" and refused to part with it until 1911, when the Detroit Institute of Arts finally prevailed upon him.

PLATE 11

UNION SQUARE IN SPRING
1896

Oil on canvas
21½" x 21½" (54.6 cm x 53.3 cm)
Smith College Museum of Art,
Northampton, Massachusetts

In 1874, Impressionism had evoked derision from the Paris art critics. The label itself is supposed to have been coined by Louis Leroy who wrote for the satirical journal *Charivari*. Its inspiration, originally meant to be derogatory, lay in the title of one of Monet's paintings shown in that first exhibition, *An Impression: Sunrise.* Another work by Monet, *Boulevard des Capucines,* caused Leroy to describe the representation of pedestrians in this street scene as 'innumerable black tongue lickings.'[7] But twenty-two years later in New York, Hassam could paint his Union Square subject with the same freedom of expressive means, and find only approval for his efforts. What had once been a radical art form was, by the turn of the century, the prevailing idiom of conservative painting in America.

To be sure, Impressionism tended to seduce the eye with decorative color, and, to this extent, it had inevitable appeal to the general public. But the compelling motive behind the success of Impressionism in late 19th-century America was that it provided certain comfortable assurances in a world in rapid transition. The "genteel tradition" in American thought was, in effect, a screen erected to mask the unpleasant realities of modern life. As Henry Steele Commager has observed,

> The decade of the nineties is the watershed of American history. . . . [This] generation . . . should have been self-confident and triumphant, for the past was reassuring and the future dazzling. The Continent had been subdued, the Republic extended to its farthest reaches—its stability established, its power acknowledged, its influence felt throughout the world. Liberty, enlightenment, and prosperity flourished. . . . Yet no previous generation had been more bedeviled by problems, and no earlier problems, except those of slavery, had seemed more vexatious. Instead of being exalted, thoughtful Americans were overwhelmed with a consciousness of questions unsolved, promises unfulfilled, and certitudes lost."[8]

American art of this period tended to gloss over those problems and to reflect an upper-middle-class world of comfort and affluence. This may be especially noted in the representations of the world of privileged womanhood, as seen through the eyes of such artists as William M. Paxton, and Hassam's colleagues of the Ten, Joseph R. De Camp, Frank W. Benson, and Edmund C. Tarbell. Though Hassam restricted himself largely to New York street scenes and New England landscapes, he was content to portray the world without subjective judgment or commentary. This would be the mission of that younger generation of realist painters, led by Robert Henri, the Ashcan School, and photographers like Lewis Hine and Jacob Riis. For Hassam, Union Square was not associated in his mind as the gathering place of trade union orators and firebrand reformers, but was a spectacle of color to be lovingly transposed to canvas. All the same, there is something akin to commentary here in the juxtaposition of the gentle, delicate forms and colors of the Square and the harsh angularity of the city's commercial architecture.

[7] John Rewald, *The History of Impressionism* (New York: The Museum of Modern Art, 1946), p. 258.
[8] Henry Steele Commager, *The American Mind* (New Haven: Yale University Press, 1953), p. 49.

PLATE 12

THE SPANISH STAIRS,
ROME
1897
Oil on canvas
29" x 23" (74 cm x 58.4 cm)
Los Angeles County Museum of Art
(William Randolph Hearst Collection)

The Hassams departed New York in the winter of 1896 and arrived in Naples in December. By January they were in Rome. Italy had been an enticement to Americans since the 18th century, when the young Benjamin West ventured forth to study painting. Some, like the 19th-century sculptor William Wetmore Story, went there as visitors and remained as expatriates. Each new generation seemed to renew a loyalty to Italy as the wellspring of Western civilization. As late as 1896, the American mural painter Edwin H. Blashfield published a newly edited version of Vasari's *Lives of the Artists,* a perennial favorite among travelers abroad.

The contrast between the "deafening present" of America, as the writer Henry James described it, and the eloquent silence of Italy's past attracted many Americans. As Van Wyck Brooks observed,

> How could there not be more travelers from a land where everything changed to the timeless world of the Pantheon, the Capitol, St. Peter's, where one could sit, in the Caffè Greco at the table Benjamin West had sat in the yesterday of Gibbon and Piranesi? In Rome, the Marble Faun still stood on the same spot in the same room where it had stood in the days of Hawthorne. Not far away within the Baths of Diocletian, the cypresses of Michelangelo still flourished. . . .

The Spanish Stairs were a part of Rome that had long inspired the great men of American letters, largely because of the picaresque figures who haunted it in the 19th century. Nathaniel Hawthorne had written about them in *The Marble Faun,* as did the sculptor Story in his *Roba di Roma.* The painter Christopher P. Cranch, writing in 1858 of Beppo, the beggar king of the Spanish Stairs, commented that he "could as little have missed old Beppo in Rome and on his old place, as I could have missed the boat fountain at the bottom of the Spanish Stairs." Hassam, too, became a devotee of the Eternal City. His painting of the Stairs avoids the pitfall of the souvenir view by concentrating on the rhythms of the forms rather than upon the significance of the well-known architecture. By treating the staccato horizontals with infinite variation, he transforms an otherwise banal subject into an arresting pattern of color cadences.

PLATE 13

TUILERIES GARDENS
1897
Oil on canvas
24¼″ x 24¼″ (60.6 cm x 60.6 cm)
The High Museum of Art, Atlanta
(Gift of Miss Mary E. Haverty for the
J.J. Haverty Collection)

For the greater part of 1897 Hassam and his wife traveled abroad. Their itinerary took them from Italy to England where Hassam painted the countryside near the River Stour. En route, they paused in France, spending some time in the popular artists' colony at Pont Aven, Brittany. Just as the region's deeply religious folk had evoked a strong response from Gauguin, so was Hassam stirred by them. A notable example, quite atypical of his usual interests, is an almost hieratic profile portrait in costume of a young peasant woman at her devotions, *Brittany, At the Pardon.* But it was in Paris that he burst into a new colorism. Not only are the Paris pictures freer—there is less dependence upon drawing—but, at last, these pictures seem to fuse drawing and painting into a single act.

Analogies to the work of Alfred Sisley and Camille Pissarro are inevitable in paintings like *Tuileries Gardens.* The spirit of Paris, its elegance which made it truly the "City of Light," is ably captured in this scintillating rendering of the north side of the great park. Here, the artist deftly suggests the gaiety of the Rue de Rivoli, with its great hotels, the Meurice and the Continental. A comparison between this picture and *Union Square in Spring* of 1896 (Plate 11) is instructive about Hassam's ability to adjust his technique to his mood. Both works are conceived in a square format for maximum emphasis upon the inter-relationships of color, and both are charged with the flickering brushwork of Hassam's mature Impressionist manner. Yet slight adjustments in the chromatic intensity of the Paris subject act to alter its ambience, creating a statement in a major key in distinction to the Union Square subject's minor key. It is not possible to mistake the Tuileries Gardens picture for anything other than a Paris scene. What is remarkable is that this is accomplished through color alone; it is color which establishes the appropriate mood. *Tuileries Gardens* is a paramount example of what Hassam meant when he said, "A picture that does not carry its own message of loveliness, but which requires the services of an artistic guide, is not, to my mind, a work of art."

PLATE 14

PONT ROYAL, PARIS
1897
Oil on canvas
24½″ x 28½″ (62 cm x 72.4 cm)
Cincinnati Art Museum
(Israel and Caroline Wilson Fund)

Hassam's return to Paris was marked by a renewed creative energy, as if physical contact with the birthplace of Impressionism had reaffirmed his chosen path in art. The paintings of 1897 possess a degree of poetic imagery and a level of technical proficiency he had never attained before. Especially in the Pont Royal subject, Hassam attained a virtuosity exemplified by an exquisitely modulated color in the extreme upper range of the value scale. In terms of its feeling for translucent atmosphere, *Pont Royal, Paris* comes closest to the work of John Twachtman, who was already abandoning representational art in favor of a formal, almost abstract, color play. Hassam, however, would subsequently pull back from this advanced position to more traditional ground.

For Hassam, representational imagery was the foundation which gave logic and order to the plastic values of art. Even in the Pont Royal painting, with its potential for sheer eye play, the artist does not deny his interest in realistic detail.

There is great precision here with respect to the scene described, as he glances out his hotel window onto the Quai Voltaire and across the Seine to the Tuileries Gardens in the distance. These seemingly casual observations take into account the cast shadows of early morning, the booksellers' stalls just opening up for the day's business, and even the impish notation of the street *pissoir*, which is at once so characteristic of Paris and so useful as a pivot point in the picture's composition.

Pont Royal, Paris was an immediate critical and financial success. Shown at the Pennsylvania Academy in 1899, it won for Hassam the coveted Temple Gold Medal; six months later it was acquired by the Cincinnati Art Museum. It is rather fitting that Hassam acknowledged the purchase of the painting, perhaps his greatest homage to French Impressionism, on the last Bastille Day of the 19th century.

PLATE 15

JULY NIGHT
1898
Oil on canvas
37" x 31" (94 cm x 79 cm)
Collection Ira M. Koger, Jackson-
ville, Florida

Upon his return from Europe in the fall of 1897, Hassam set about forming an independent group of Impressionist artists, who called themselves the Ten American Painters. (See pp. 16–17 for a brief history of the Ten.) At the heart of their schism with the New York art establishment was their sympathy with the ideals of the influential Esthetic Movement. The inaugural exhibition of the Ten was held in March 1898; it served to identify Hassam and his colleagues as artists committed to saving American Impressionism from the state of atrophy into which it was rapidly falling.

Hassam probably observed some of the more advanced forms of French painting during his stay in Paris in 1897, and subtly blended some of those influences with his own sensibilities. Formulating theories about art and the systematic exploration of these theories were never of particular interest to American painters. However, the advent of the Ten just at the moment Hassam returned from Europe seems significant. The Ten's concern for a more rigorous formal association with the principles of the Esthetic Movement may have had its origin in the general ferment of international art at the time. Certainly Hassam's *July Night*, probably painted in the summer of 1898, suggests a new and strong element at work in his art. Not only is the painting's composition dominated by the occult balance as-

sociated with *japonisme*—an especially important element in the theories of the Esthetic Movement—but its method of execution is suffused with a particularly energetic pointillist technique. Pointillism, or more properly "divisionism," was a refinement of the broken color experiments of the Impressionists. It sought to achieve a more reliable method for ordering color into optical mixtures, and is associated with the work of the French post-Impressionism. The almost iridescent colors employed by Hassam in this painting depart radically from his usual palette. These, together with the dreamlike mood of the subject, push the work beyond the limits of Impressionism altogether. Indeed, the total effect of *July Night* is strikingly similar to the late work of one of the leaders of post-Impressionism, Georges Seurat.[9] While *July Night* may argue plausibly for the momentary influence of postimpressionism in Hassam's art, it is really the result of a synthesis of a number of parallel influences, chief of which is that particularly American manifestation of the Esthtic Movement, Tonalism.

The setting for this painting is the garden of the house on Egypt Lane in East Hampton that the Hassams eventually acquired in 1920. Maude Hassam posed for the work, which remained one of the artist's cherished possessions until his death, when it reverted to the American Academy of Arts and Letters.

[9] A revealing comparison can be made to such late work of Seurat as *Singer at the Café Concert*, ca. 1887. Illustrated in John Rewald, *Post-Impressionism* (New York: The Museum of Modern Art, 1956), p. 429.

PLATE 16

GLOUCESTER HARBOR
1899
Oil on canvas
24½" x 22½" (62 cm x 56.2 cm)
Steven Straw Company

Since the mid-19th century, Gloucester and Rockport on Cape Ann have provided artists with scenic motifs that have become firmly imbedded in the iconography of American art. Fitz Hugh Lane's airy luminist panoramas of Gloucester Harbor became known to a wide audience in the 1850's through lithographic reproductions. Later, in 1873 and again in 1880, Winslow Homer chose Gloucester as a proving ground for his early work in watercolor. Both artists were attracted to the special quality of Gloucester's light. As Barbara Novak has observed, "the climate, geography and topography of the town of Gloucester ... contributed to certain architectonic luminist qualities in Homer's works," as they did in Lane's.

Hassam had his first encounter with Gloucester during a summer trip to New England in 1890, just after his return from Europe. He responded by painting *Yachts, Gloucester Harbor* (San Francisco Art Institute), a sun-drenched view of the harbor filled with the white sails of boats. Almost a decade passed before he was again in Gloucester, and by that time, Hassam's style had fully emerged. The former discrepancies in brushwork, which can be noted in foreground and background passages of the 1890 pic-

ture, had now been resolved to a unity—paint is applied in energetic color strokes that bind the work into a kind of tapestry effect. The square format of his canvas is used here again to emphasize the formal interrelationships of color and the elements of composition.

John H. Twachtman took nearly the same point of view in his *Gloucester Harbor*, (ca. 1900; Canajoharie Library and Art Gallery). Indeed, for a brief time, Hassam's and Twachtman's styles seemed to merge. Their association as members of the Ten American Painters group, founded in 1897, was undoubtedly responsible for this affinity. Hassam appreciated the painterly perceptions of his colleague, noting in 1903,

> The great beauty of design which is conspicuous in Twachtman's paintings is what impressed me always; and it is apparent to all who see ... that his works were ... strong, and at the same time delicate even to evasiveness. . . .

It is curious to observe that Hassam never altered his conception of this 1899 Gloucester motif. He repeated his performance with almost no change in either composition or color harmonies in a 1909 painting *Gloucester Harbor* (Norton Gallery of Art, West Palm Beach).

PLATE 17

LATE AFTERNOON,
WINTER, NEW YORK
1900
Oil on canvas
37¼" x 29⅛" (94.6 cm x 74 cm)
The Brooklyn Museum
(Dick S. Ramsay Fund)

By the turn of the century, the city had become a dominant factor in American life. The nation's foremost metropolis, then as now, was New York. In 1900, almost three and a half million people lived and worked there, the result of the unification of Manhattan with its four neighboring boroughs. New York was a place of unprecedented change and activity as new and larger buildings and bridges quickly altered the city's skyline. Daniel Burham's Flatiron Building of 1902 became the city's first skyscraper, and teams of architects planned model tenement developments to house the incoming waves of immigrants. By the turn of the century, commercial electric lighting, begun by Thomas Edison in the financial district in the 1880's, was a commonplace, as were the "elevated railroads." In 1900, New Yorkers saw the first automobile show, a harbinger of what was to come seven years later—motorbuses replaced horse-drawn stages on Fifth Avenue.

In this era of turbulent change, American artists responded to the stimuli of the city in different ways. To those realist painters led by Robert Henri—the so-called Ashcan School—the sometimes squalid aspects of life in New York offered a rich vein of material. Jacob Riis, the Danish immigrant who became the photographer-chronicler of New York's sordid Lower East Side, wrote, "New York is a queer town. The grist of every hopper in the world comes to it." Yet there were other painters and photographers who chose to see the city as a place of romantic imagery. One writer, O. Henry, compared it to an Arabian Nights experience, full of "palaces, ba-

zaars, khans and byways." This tendency to transform the prosaic urban scene into something infinitely romantic probably had its inception with the Esthetic Movement. The "nocturnes" of James A. M. Whistler were especially influential, as was his manifesto, the celebrated "Ten O'Clock" lecture which proclaimed,

> . . . [W]hen the evening mist clothes the riverside with poetry, as with a veil, and the poor buildings lose themselves in the dim sky, and the tall chimneys become campanili, and the warehouses are palaces in the night, and the whole city hangs in the heavens, and fairy-land is before us . . . nature, who, for once, has sung in tune, sings her exquisite song to the artist alone, her son and her master. . . .

For a brief time around 1900, a number of painters and photographers—Hassam and Alfred Stieglitz among them—revived the tonalist approach to art by shifting the former emphasis of tonalism away from the natural landscape of the countryside to the man-made cityscape.

Hassam has been called the "Sisley of Madison Avenue." No example of his work better illustrates that comparison than *Late Afternoon, Winter, New York*. In retrospect, Hassam's momentary return to tonalism, which he had abandoned in the 1880's, seems to be less a concession to the Esthetic Movement than a genuine response to a specific set of visual phenomena. The sustained high color key of *Late Afternoon*, and its uniformly even brushwork, points the picture more toward abstraction and the future of art, than to the past.

PLATE 18

AFTERNOON
1900
Oil on canvas
18" x 23" (45.7 cm x 58.4 cm)
Collection Mrs. John D. Rockefeller III

During the summer of 1900, Hassam painted at Provincetown, Massachusetts. It was his third painting trip to New England in as many summers, but his first visit to this particular place. What may have attracted him there was the artist colony established in Provincetown in 1899 by Charles Webster Hawthorne, a talented pupil of Hassam's old friend William Merritt Chase. Hawthorne's infectious enthusiasm easily attracted students to his Cape Cod School of Art. This is evident in the tone of the School's brochure:

> Huddled under the immense sand dunes at the extreme end of Cape Cod is Provincetown. . . . it is only occasionally that the traveller comes upon this oldest and most picturesque fishing hamlet on the New England coast. It seems impossible to realize when first setting foot in the village, that one is only three or four hours from Boston. For the very reason of its obscure position, Provincetown has kept its refreshingly primitive character, not having been rendered colorless by the inroads of summer excursionists. . . . nets, boats and tackle . . . form a jumble of color in the intense sunlight accentuated by the brilliant blue of the harbor. . . . Beyond, the dunes rise to an imposing height, and are covered with the bayberry and the stunted oak, with patches of white sand. . . .

Although Hassam was never dependent upon associations with other artists, his natural conviviality drew him to various places where painters gathered, especially during the summers— Appledore was the first, and later there was Cos Cob, Connecticut, and East Hampton, Long Island.

Afternoon is neither signed nor dated. Originally, the subject was thought to be Nantucket, but Hassam never visited this famous whaling town south of Cape Cod. The picture does contain an interesting clue pointing to Provincetown as the scene represented: on the horizon are shown low-lying dunes with waves breaking on the shoreline. These correspond exactly to the position of the hook of Cape Cod extending southward from Race Point, relative to the town itself. In this painting, Hassam restates a familiar theme, his wife seated among flowers. It is a subject that he essayed eleven years before in *Mrs. Hassam in Their Garden* (Plate 6). Once again he chose afternoon, with its lengthening shadows and mellow sunlight, so redolent of the artist's innate romanticism.

PLATE 19

COAST SCENE, ISLES
OF SHOALS
1901
Oil on canvas
25" x 30⅛" (63.5 cm x 76.5 cm)
The Metropolitan Museum of Art
(Gift of George A. Hearn, 1909)

Appledore and the other Isles of Shoals provided Hassam with an elemental landscape he could find nowhere else in his summer painting excursions. One of a group of nine small islands lying some ten miles off the Maine-New Hampshire coast, it derives its name from the 18th-century English fishermen from the village of Appledore in Devon who first settled there. The collective title of the islands refers to the shoals of fish that were formerly plentiful there. Hassam always viewed Appledore as a formative influence on his art, and a place of happy associations. There he met George Chadwick, the composer, who bought the first picture Hassam ever offered for sale. Later, through the doyenne of Appledore, Celia Thaxter, he met such noted men of letters as Richard Watson Gilder, editor of *Century* magazine, and the poet James Russell Lowell.

From his first encounter with the Isles in the summer of 1890 until his final visit there in 1916, Hassam repeatedly explored the motif of rudimentary rock forms and sea that are the dominant features of the landscape. His work there bears comparison with Monet's paintings of the Britanny coast. However, instead of painting the same subject in varying conditions of light, as was the tendency of the French Impressionists, Hassam concentrated upon a single quality of light throughout his many different Appledore pictures. Noon was the time of day Hassam chose most often to represent, with its broad, overhead light that flattens the forms of nature. Nearly without exception, Hassam's Appledore pictures establish a very high horizon line, so high that the sky is almost excluded. Emphasis is firmly placed on the solidity of nature, rather than its voids. A similar picture, *Coast Scene, Northeast Headlands* (Corcoran Gallery of Art, Washington, D.C.), also painted in 1901, reveals the artist experimenting with different compositional devices: the enclosed space of the work illustrated here shifts to a more open, and perhaps more randomly chosen, arrangement in the other work. Toward the end of the decade, Hassam tended to inject the element of the figure into his Appledore pictures. This, unfortunately, mitigated the expressive power invested in the stark simplicity of their basic rock and sea motifs.

PLATE 20

THE MESSENGER BOY
1903

Oil on canvas
18¼" x 32¼" (45.4 cm x 81.9 cm)
Museum of Art, Rhode Island School
of Design
(Jesse H. Metcalf Fund)

Hassam had long admired the work of James A. M. Whistler, which he probably saw in depth for the first time during his 1883 visit to London. According to Adeline Adams, on his return trip from Paris to New York in 1889, Hassam paused in London and "drew and painted street scenes. . . . Long an admirer of Whistler's art, he found a wealth of outdoor themes in Old Chelsea, and along the Thames embankment. . . ." *The Messenger Boy* owes a particular debt to Whistler's pictorial style, and it is a curious fact that this painting, the first in Hassam's *oeuvre* to demonstrate such a forthright attachment, was created the year of Whistler's death. The two men never met, and when Hassam learned of Whistler's death, he expressed his regret at never having done so. Comparisons abound, but a particularly apt correlation with Whistler's work can be found in this artist's 1878 *Nocturne in Gray and Gold: Chelsea Snow* (Fogg Art Museum, Cambridge)—it is complete even to the notation of the lonely figure trudging in the snow.

Four years before, Hassam had painted a very similar figure in a more conventional street scene, *Fifth Avenue in Winter* (Museum of Art, Carnegie Institute, Pittsburgh). This painting is distinguished by its emphasis upon deep space and by its descriptive detail of carriages and town house architecture. The 1903 work seems to sweep aside any such interest in favor of a play with pictorial arrangement. In the 1903 performance, it is only by throwing the street into a slight perspective that Hassam appears to retreat from a full commitment to a Whistlerian "arrangement." Indeed, if one were to eliminate the bottom half of *The Messenger Boy* the effect would be a nearly abstract play upon horizontal rectangles. Hassam's use of tightly controlled color harmonies, within the range of the near complements of blue and yellow, adds to the essentially abstract feeling of this work.

On an historical level, *The Messenger Boy* embraces the very subject matter of the humble life of New York's streets that was being espoused by Robert Henri's group of realist painters. Henri's *West 57th Street* (Yale University Art Gallery, New Haven), painted in 1902, makes an especially apt comparison with Hassam's picture. It demonstrates that Hassam, contrary to the conventional wisdom, was not merely an Impressionist artist associated with the "genteel tradition," but was as fully conversant with the vocabulary of realism as were Henri and his colleagues of the Eight.

PLATE 21

THE HOVEL AND THE
SKYSCRAPER
1904

Oil on canvas
35" x 31" (88.9 cm x 78.7 cm)
Collection Mr. and Mrs. Meyer Po-
tamkin

Shortly after the turn of the century, the Hassams moved from West 57th Street to a new apartment studio at 27 West 67th Street. This building was one of those erected on 67th Street expressly for artists, and combined residential and studio space. The move brought Hassam into contact not only with the more ethnically colorful neighborhood of the upper West Side, as *The Messenger Boy* (Plate 20) attests, but also placed him in the midst of the dynamism of New York's prodigious growth. While the fashionable East Side was being adorned with public art—St. Gaudens's heroic equestrian bronze sculpture of General Sherman was unveiled at the 59th Street and Fifth Avenue entrance to Central Park in 1903—the West Side celebrated the opening of a new subway line in 1904.

A glimpse of the dynamic quality of New York life is provided by *The Hovel and the Skyscraper*. The title of the painting is merely symbolic in this respect. The construction going on in the foreground represents a new parish house for a church building at the corner of West 68th Street and Central Park West, while the "hovel" in the middle distance is actually the old riding stables at the West 67th Street entrance to Central Park. This view was probably one that Hassam encountered daily from the windows of his studio at the rear of the building. The work is not as chromatically brilliant as George Bellows's series of paintings chronicling the birth of Pennsylvania Station, such as his 1909 *Pennsylvania Station Excavation* (Brooklyn Museum, New York). Nevertheless, Hassam's tonal inventions in this picture more perfectly marry the spirit of Impressionism to the mood of his times than any other single work by him. The hard angularity of the foreground forms, with their darker colors, contrasts abruptly with the soft, undulating landscape of the Park. All in all, the composition makes a bold statement about that often disconcerting phenomenon of the New York scene—its ceaseless change.

PLATE 22

GIANT MAGNOLIAS
1904
Oil on canvas
35" x 20" (88.9 cm x 50.8 cm)
Reynold House Collection, Winston-Salem, North Carolina

Inherent in the art of still-life painting is a degree of precision in the rendering of forms. The uses of Impressionism, therefore, seem ill-suited to this branch of art. Indeed, of all the artists in the circle of the French Impressionists, only Henri Fantin-Latour, who never really shared their way of seeing, made any significant contribution to still-life painting. Of course, Claude Monet and Pierre Renoir occasionally produced still lifes, but these are only peripheral to their art. Impressionism celebrates the atmosphere of nature, and thus, the Impressionists found their most agreeable métier in landscape painting. The table top world of the still life precludes almost any possibility for capturing the nuances of light that occur with the depth of field in landscapes. And the softness of focus that is one of the charms of Impressionist painting seems almost illogical when applied to still life. Yet precisely because American art has always been strong when dealing with the problems of objective realism, even its Impressionist painters could successfully adjust to the requirements of the still-life subject.

Of Hassam's contemporaries, William Merritt Chase was the most notable exponent of the still-life painting, although he remarked that "there is nothing more difficult [to paint] than flowers." Hassam himself attempted only a few flower subjects. *Giant Magnolias* is certainly the most heroic of all of them, in terms of physical size of the canvas and monumentality of vision. As early as 1892, Hassam approached the problem of flower painting in a close-up study of a field of poppies at Appledore, on the Isles of Shoals. That was essentially a watercolor exercise; and despite the implied space in the picture and his use of a brilliant palette, the effect of the Appledore work is flat. On the other hand, the solid modeling and the deep, lustrous tonalities of *Giant Magnolias* relate the picture more to traditional modes of still-life painting than to Impressionism. As if aware of the problem of losing the characteristic blond palette—a problem inherent in painting any interior subject—Hassam quickly returned to a higher color key in *Still Life with Fruits* (Portland Art Museum, Oregon), also painted in 1904. From this time through the early 1920's, when his interest in still life virtually ceased, Hassam consistently used a high-keyed palette for this subject.

PLATE 23

CHURCH AT OLD LYME
1906
Oil on canvas
30⅛" x 25¼" (76.5 cm x 64.1 cm)
Parrish Art Museum, Southampton,
New York
(Gift of Mrs. Robert M. Littlejohn)

Around the turn of the century, the village of Old Lyme, Connecticut, became a kind of summer academy of American Impressionism. Frank Vincent DuMond and Henry Ward Ranger, both well-known and respected members of the faculty of the National Academy of Design and the Art Students League in New York, were regular summer residents, as were Chauncey Ryder, Guy Carleton Wiggins, and Walter Griffin. The "Old Lyme Colony", as the summer artist population was known, had been spontaneously generated by the warm hospitality of Miss Florence Griswold, a descendent of one of Old Lyme's distinguished families. The Griswold house accepted boarders within its spacious confines, and it eventually became the heart of the colony as artists and their families returned year after year to occupy the same quarters. An occasional visitor was Willard L. Metcalf, one of Hassam's colleagues of the Ten, who would stop at Old Lyme en route from New York to his summer studio at Chester, Vermont. In 1906, Metcalf painted *May Night* (Corcoran Gallery of Art, Washington, D.C.), an ethereal moonlit landscape showing the columned porch of the Griswold house, a kind of reverie to the gracious life shared by the artists of Old Lyme.

For several seasons prior to his first visit to Old Lyme in 1903, Hassam sampled various locations in southern New England: Provincetown, Massachusetts; Newport, Rhode Island; and New Canaan, Connecticut. With his discovery of Old Lyme, his wanderings ceased, and for four summers, he returned to this little town on the Connecticut River, with its heritage of handsome Federal architecture and its gentle landscape. The old Congregational Church on the town's main street became a popular subject for Hassam. Two versions exist from that first summer of 1903 (Albright-Knox Museum, Buffalo; Collection of Mr. and Mrs. Irving Mitchell Felt). There is a singular consistency among all the variations, each conceived as a strikingly simple arrangement of white, gold, and blue. The strength and simplicity of the Old Lyme church series is symbolic of the values in life which Hassam cherished. The country village became for Hassam and his friends at Old Lyme an antidote to the increasing turmoil and change of urban existence.

PLATE 24

BEDFORD HILLS
1908
Oil on canvas
22" x 26" (55.9 cm x 66 cm)
Akron Art Institute, Akron, Ohio
(Gift of Edwin C. Shaw)

The landscape of southern New England held personal associations for Hassam that seem to invest his paintings of that region with a special warmth of color and freshness of style. Hassam had been especially close to John H. Twachtman, and he and Maude frequently visited Twachtman and his wife at their house, Holly Farm, near Greenwich, Connecticut. Another colleague of the Ten, J. Alden Weir, lived in a handsome little house at Branchville in central Connecticut. Yet another friend, the illustrator and painter of the American West, Frederic Remington, lived at Ridgefield, Connecticut, surrounded by the artifacts of Plains Indian cultures. Remington provided the Hassams with expansive hospitality during their frequent visits, treating them to western-style horseback rides over the tamed pastures of Ridgefield.

It was probably on one of these visits to Ridgefield that Hassam painted *Bedford Hills*. In 1922, when the painting was sold by one collector to another, Hassam wrote to Edwin C. Shaw, the new owner, "The canvas was painted in the old town of Bedford, Westchester County, New York. It is, it seems to me, as good a piece of painting as I have done of a small landscape. It is unquestionably a painter's picture, and for that reason alone is a collector's picture. . . ." In its feeling for the radiant light and stillness of a New England summer day, *Bedford Hills* is remarkably similar to pictures painted that same summer by J. Alden Weir, *Building a Dam, Shetucket River* (Cleveland Museum of Art), and by Willard Metcalf, *Twin Birches* (Pennsylvania Academy of the Fine Arts, Philadelphia). One is struck by the vitality of the works of the leading practitioners of American Impressionism during this period. Far from being in a state of senescence, Impressionism in the hands of talents like Hassam, Weir, and Metcalf achieved a high level of pictorial invention and poetic creativity.

PLATE 25

BRIDGE AT OLD LYME
1908
Oil on canvas
24" x 27" (60.9 cm x 68.6 cm)
Georgia Museum of Art, The University of Georgia, Athens
(Gift of Alfred H. Holbrook)

Hassam's sense of the historical development of modern art persuaded him that French Impressionism was really born in England. He believed that "the whole modern movement . . . in painting was due to English artists—Constable, Girtin, Turner, Bonington, and all the English water color painters who were first to work out-of-doors with a clear palette." Delacroix had been influenced by seeing the work of Constable in the Paris Salon of 1824. Later, during the Commune of 1870, Monet had fled Paris for London where he, too, came under the spell of Constable, as well as of Turner. Even before Hassam had made his first trip to Europe, Impressionism was flourishing in Britain under the aegis of the New English Art Club, and James A. M. Whistler was astonishing London audiences with his daring tonal paintings which he called "arrangements," "symphonies," and "nocturnes."

It is not surprising, then, that *Bridge at Old Lyme* partakes of a very strong flavor of English painting. One is reminded of certain works by John Constable, such as his *Stoke-by-Nayland* (Art Institute of Chicago), where the eye is drawn into a lush landscape dominated by a powerful sky. The romantic image of the solitary hunter with his hound points to an earlier age of painting, as well. Yet Hassam's richly applied, scintillating color harmonies of ultramarine blue, yellow greens, and umber accents proclaim a sensibility that has also absorbed some of the lessons of modernism.

PLATE 26

**AFTERNOON SKY,
HARNEY DESERT**
1908
Oil on canvas
20⅛" x 30⅛" (51.1 cm x 76.5 cm)
Portland Art Museum, Portland, Oregon
(Gift of August Berg, Henrietta E. Failing, Winslow B. Ayer, William D. Wheelwright, I. N. Fleischner, and the Estate of D. P. Thompson)

In the fall of 1908, Hassam departed the familiar New England countryside, and traveled West for the first time. He arrived in San Francisco on the Union-Pacific Railroad, having made the transcontinental crossing alone; Maude remained in the East. The object of this trip was to fulfill a commission for a mural decoration in the Portland, Oregon, residence of Colonel and Mrs. Charles Erskine Scott Wood. A contemporary described Colonel Wood as a person of "vitality, magnetism, charm, wit and teasing irreverence," and his house a place that contained "all the Arts: painting, sculpture, literature, creativeness—hospitality." Hassam provided a sunlit frieze for the upper walls of the library, which was unique in that section of the country, not only for its size, but for its rare contents. Obviously, Hassam had found a kindred spirit in Colonel Wood, as well as a patron.

Hassam stayed in Oregon after the mural decoration was installed. Wood, whose love of the outdoors matched his love of the contemplative life, persuaded Hassam to join him on a trip to the southern portion of the state, where the land opened up into great stretches of flat country known as the Harney Desert. Signing a postcard "Marco Polo Muley Hassam" (Remington had given him the sobriquet "Muley"), Hassam wrote to Maude at home in New York:

> 200 miles in the desert with Wood. Trout a thousand miles long. Mallard ducks so thick they knock your hat off when you put your head out of cover. Venison hoe cake and alfalfa honey. . . .

The joyousness implicit in this message is transmitted directly in pictorial terms through the radiance of *Afternoon Sky, Harney Desert.* The semi-arid expanse of sagebrush and the low-lying hills are crowned with glorious cloud forms that convey the artist's sense of profound elation in the presence of a vision of nature that was new to him. Very likely, Hassam's perceptions of this strange and overpowering landscape were heightened by Wood's own sensitivity to it. Wood found the Oregon desert country a transcendent life experience, to which he responded in what he called his "desert sonnets."

> The Desert is a beauteous bride to me,
> Patient and unseeking, lone she stands,
> In all her grace and naked majesty,
>
> Her robes, the skies, unto the zenith torn,
> With gold and purple and the day dawn's fire,
> And all the triumph of the flowing morn.

Years later, writing a letter of sympathy to Maude upon learning of Hassam's death, Wood remembered "the journeys into the desert, the . . . light . . . he so fully appreciated and as Weir said when he was also there with me later— 'Muley was the only man able to get it—I can't do it.'"

PLATE 27

THE CHINESE MERCHANTS
1909
Oil on canvas
19⅞" x 36" (51.5 cm x 91.4 cm)
Freer Gallery of Art, Smithsonian Institution, Washington, D.C.

During his visit to Portland, Oregon, Hassam visited the Chinese quarter of the city. The oriental flavor of life there must have suggested the format of this painting, but it was not the first time that he had composed a street scene in a long horizontal. *The Messenger Boy* (Plate 20) of six years earlier is conceived in much the same way. However, *The Chinese Merchants* carries to complete assimilation the design principles espoused by James A. M. Whistler in his "arrangements." This work is unusual in Hassam's *oeuvre*, not only because it does not conceptually connect very strongly with his other paintings, but also because it seems so overtly Whistlerian.

It has been suggested that *The Chinese Merchants* was a calculated gesture toward attracting the patronage of the prominent Detroit industrialist, Charles Lang Freer. Under the guidance of Ernest Fenollosa, the art connoisseur and philosopher, Freer had assembled one of the country's most extensive collections of Oriental art. In addition, Freer held a special regard for such American painters of the tonalist persuasion as Dwight Tryon, whose work he began buying in 1889. He gradually added pictures by Abbott H. Thayer and Thomas W. Dewing, and in 1903, crowned his collection of American art with the purchase of Whistler's *The Princess of the Land of Porcelain.* Freer was especially fond of Whistler's paintings, and had assembled a large group of these by the time he offered his collection to the nation. This extraordinary gift was accepted officially by the United States government in 1906; it was the first significant donation of art to the nation by a private individual.

As early as 1905, Freer had been approached to buy a painting of Hassam's. The offer was declined by the collector in a letter to E. H. Carqueville, in which he wrote,

> . . . [W]hile I have the highest regard for the work of Childe Hassam, who, by the way, is a friend of mine, I have not as yet included any of his work in my collection, and for the present at least, I am not prepared to consider buying any of his pictures.

Hassam, on his side, was by this time aware of the advantage that would accrue if museums were to purchase his paintings. Writing to L. E. Rowe, the director of the Museum of Art, Rhode Island School of Design, he accepted a lesser figure for *The Messenger Boy* with the observation, "I shall of course be very glad to be represented in your collection, *which will do an immense amount of good*" (emphasis added). The prospect of being represented in a collection in the nation's capital may well have inspired Hassam to study Freer's taste. However that may be, Hassam's dealer, N. E. Montross, mounted an exhibition in April 1909, "Paintings of Eastern Oregon by Childe Hassam," and by the following April, Freer had, at last, become "prepared to consider" the purchase of a Hassam painting.

PLATE 28

THE FRENCH TEA GARDEN
1910

Oil on canvas
35" x 40" (88.9 cm x 101.6 cm)
Hunter Museum of Art, Chattanooga,
Tennessee

In the summer of 1910, the Hassams made their final trip to Europe. Their itinerary was similar to that of 1897, except that they omitted Italy. Writing from his Paris hotel, the Empire on the Rue Daunou, Hassam informed Weir, who was in Branchville that summer,

> We have been in Paris for two weeks and we are about to move on to the Côte du Nord by the sea. . . . We had fine weather in London, cold in Holland. . . . I made a 14th July [painting] from the balcony here.

While this painting, *July 14th, Rue Daunou* (Metropolitan Museum of Art) was the seed that would blossom six years later into the first of his *Flag Series* of Fifth Avenue, New York, Hassam's output in 1910 continued to concentrate upon more familiar themes. Landscapes, such as *Road to the Land of Nod* (Beinecke Rare Book Library, Yale University, New Haven), and figure subjects, like his brilliant study of the effects of light in *Contre Jour* (Chicago Art Institute), reveal no marked changes in either his technique or his color harmonies. However, while still in France that year, Hassam painted one picture resonant with a color and mood that is not quite consistent with his usual manner—*The French Tea Garden.*

In 1906, the highly acclaimed American painter Frederick Frieseke acquired a house at Giverny where his immediate neighbor was Claude Monet. Gradually, Frieseke's style changed from a dark, painterly realism to the *plein air* manner of Impressionism. By 1908, when he won a prize in the Corcoran Gallery of Art's prestigious 2nd Biennial Exhibition, Frieseke was becoming well known in America. Although Hassam never met Monet, and it is uncertain whether he ever knew Frieseke, he could not have been ignorant of the work of either. Even a cursory study of *The French Tea Garden* will reveal that Hassam here had adjusted his palette toward a more decorative color scheme than was his usual practice, and away from his customarily more muted range of color. In this painting, his choice of certain yellow greens, pinks, and pale blues finds specific echoes in the work of Frieseke. At the same time, Hassam puts the impress of his own temperament upon the picture, for it is strongly related to such earlier garden scenes as *Mrs. Hassam in Their Garden* (Plate 6).

PLATE 29

THE NEW YORK WINDOW
1912

Oil on canvas
45½" x 35" (115.6 cm x 88.9 cm)
The Corcoran Gallery of Art, Washington, D.C.

About 1910, Hassam took up the theme of the female figure, posed in diaphanous costume against a blacklighted window. A painting from that year, *Contre Jour* (Chicago Art Institute), even uses the French term, meaning "against the light," for its title. During the decade that followed, he created a sequence of variations on this theme that became known as the *New York Window Series.* In choosing this theme, he was working in the mainstream of academic painting of his day. By the turn of the century, the subject of the American woman of leisure had become one of the dominant elements in the *oeuvre* of conservative painters. Among Hassam's colleagues in the Ten, Benson, De Camp, Dewing, Reid, and Tarbell all were prodigious in their output of ambitious Salon paintings representing the ideal American woman.

The widespread manifestation of this theme in American art may be traced to the culture's social values and mores. As the so-called Gilded Age of the late 19th century proclaimed its outright devotion to materialism, the American woman of privilege, whose traditional tasks were being subverted by technology, exchanged her accustomed role as guardian of homely virtues for a more ornamental place in society. As the historian Ray Ginger has observed,

> Woman was free, and knew not how to use her freedom. With sparkling wit and glittering jewels, she found no men fit to admire her and had 'no place but the theatre or the streets to decorate.' Like American men, she had married machinery. She was surprised when anybody regarded her as sexual.

The most perfect representation of the emancipated woman who could find "no man fit to admire her" was created by Charles Dana Gibson, whose widely published illustrations provided a fascinated public with a new national symbol—the "Gibson Girl."

Consciously or not, American painters seemed bent upon restoring the American woman to a position of unassailable virtue, associating her with symbols of purity. Samuel Isham remarked at the time that Americans

> . . . have no goddesses or saints, they have forgotten their legends, they do not read the poets, but something of what goddess, saint, or heroine represented to other races they find in the idealization of their womankind. They will have such idealization decorous; there is no room for the note of unrestrained passion, still less for sensuality. It is the grace of children, the tenderness of motherhood, the beauty and purity of young girls which they demand, but especially the last. The American girl is placed upon a pedestal and each offers worship according to his abilities, the artist among the rest.

Hassam's "worship" tended to be restrained, and he was not inclined to burden his *New York Window* pictures with sentiment. Rarely did he particularize the features of his subjects. Rather, he offers the figure as an element in the whole composition. In *The New York Window,* the figure receives no greater articulation than does the bowl of fruit placed beside her. A comparison with *The Breakfast Room, Winter Morning, New York* (Worcester Art Museum), of a year earlier, reveals that the emphasis in these pictures is placed more on the quality of light and the mood established through color than upon ideas concerning the feminine mystique. Yet it is precisely because Hassam does not rely upon literary association, and because he hews rigorously to the formal values of art, that the *New York Window* paintings are, for the most part, superior to the efforts of most American painters of the period who indulged in this genre. The noted collector John Gellatly, who owned *Tanagra* (National Collection of Fine Art, Washington, D.C.), one of the *New York Window Series,* accurately perceived Hassam's intent. He wrote,

> It seems to me that no painter's brush has more truly met the command recorded in the Book of Genesis, "Let there be light," than yours. This you have done with truth and charm and poetry. . . .

PLATE 30

SOUTH LEDGES,
APPLEDORE
1913

Oil on canvas
34¼" x 36" (87.04 cm x 91.4 cm)
National Collection of Fine Arts,
Smithsonian Institution, Washington,
D.C.
(Gift of John Gellatly)

Sunny Blue Sea is Hassam's only major Appledore seascape that includes the human figure in a plausible relationship with nature. By and large, the Appledore paintings are devoid of figural representation, but when Hassam chose to inject the figure, he often succumbed to the notion of the "classical" nude. This weakness can be seen in the large standing female figure in *Nude, Appledore, Isles of Shoals* (Columbus Gallery of Fine Arts, Columbus) of the same year. In *Sunny* which seems to have been composed in the studio, rather than being a product of direct observation. It used as its basis *The North Gorge, Appledore, Isles of Shoals* [Columbus Gallery of Fine Arts, Columbus] of the same year. In *Sunny Blue Sea* Hassam arrived at an equitable balance between his growing tendency to concentrate upon the figure in painting and the requirements of plein air realism.

In looking at Hassam's many Appledore seascapes, it is possible to discern a subtle progression toward simplification of forms and color, and a consequent flattening of pictorial space. A comparison between *Coast Scene, Isles of Shoals* (Plate 19) of a dozen years earlier and *Sunny Blue Sea* is instructive about the changes that had gradually occurred in Hassam's art over the decade. While the earlier picture rests firmly on traditional means, the forms are articulated through strong accents of light and dark color values, *Sunny Blue Sea,* with its simplified, almost schematic composition and consistently narrow range of values, points toward a more modern approach to painting. Hassam's tendency toward a more modern statement can be seen in an intermediate work employing a similar subject, *Duck Island* (Dallas Museum of Fine Arts), painted in 1906.

Sunny Blue Sea was painted during the summer of 1913, the year of the Armory Show, and its radical departure from Hassam's usual pictorial composition may reflect a subtle assimilation of more modern tendencies in art. Here, he returns to the square format, which serves to emphasize the strong diagonal separating the picture into two, nearly equal, triangles. In terms of color, the abstract quality of this composition is reinforced by grouping whites, tans, and blues into separate, well-defined areas. Even the figure in the foreground serves to strengthen this idea—the figure merges with the surrounding rocks rather than being set in contrast to them. The thin band of sky at the extreme upper edge of the picture, with its single note of white denoting a boat on the horizon, effectively arrests the diagonal, while at the same time establishing a dynamic tension between foreground and background. Yet in truth, all considerations for the mechanics of picture making must take second place to the artist's poetic sensibilities here. Gellatly's words of appreciation for Hassam's abilities to evoke the palpable sensations of nature and his mastery of the brilliant effects of light are nowhere more appropriate than when we approach this canvas.

PLATE 31

UNION JACK, NEW YORK, APRIL MORN
1918
Oil on canvas
37" x 30" (93.9 cm x 76.2 cm)
The Joseph H. Hirshhorn Museum and Sculpture Garden, Smithsonian Institution, Washington, D.C.

The inception of Hassam's *Flag Series* paintings began in Paris in 1910 when he painted *July 14th, Rue Daunou* (Metropolitan Museum of Art). This view from his hotel window took as its subject the street below, crowded with Bastille Day celebrants and decorated with masses of the French tricolor flag. Even before the United States entered World War I, Hassam had essayed the flag theme, directly transposing the holiday spirit of his Rue Daunou subject to a New York setting in *Fourth of July, 1916* (Private Collection, New York). With the declaration of War in April 1917, Hassam was inspired by patriotic fervor to create the first of some two dozen works on the theme of the flags of the Allied powers, *Allies Day, May, 1917* (National Gallery of Art, Washington, D.C.). The scene depicted in most of these paintings is Fifth Avenue, which had become New York's traditional route for ceremonial parades. As S. C. Burchell has described it:

> More than simply the playground of the rich, the Avenue was a focus for many events important in the history of the country. A precedent was long established; on April 25, 1865, the body of Abraham Lincoln had been carried solemnly along the Avenue from Fourteenth Street to Thirty-fourth Street. And in the years that followed there were similar processions for other famous Americans: Admiral Farragut and Horace Greeley and U. S. Grant and General Sherman. By the last decades of the nineteenth century, the great parades of national groups were under way as well—the Irish, who had marched on St. Patrick's Day since Revolutionary times, and the Spanish and the Italians and the Hungarians and so many others of the melting pot. Fifth Avenue had watched innumerable other marching men, too—American soldiers and sailors and marines returning in victory from faraway battles.

Among Hassam's papers, preserved by the American Academy of Arts and Letters, there is a large collection of newspaper clippings concerning the War. Though these are unrelated to the artist's work, they are revealing about his sense of patriotism. In May 1917, he donated a number of his paintings to be sold for the benefit of a War relief fund. Even his landscape paintings of the period sometimes included references to the War. For example, *East Gloucester in War Time* (Private Collection, Oxnard, California) includes the figure of a soldier in uniform. Thus, when the United States entered the War in 1917, and it became the custom along Fifth Avenue to display the banners of the Allies, Hassam seized the opportunity to make a contribution in his own way.

Union Jack, New York, April Morn commemorates the first anniversary of the American entry into the War. By placing the flag of the United States behind that of Great Britain, the artist has symbolically suggested the aid given by America to its ally. In this picture, as in the majority of the others of the series, the brilliant geometry of the flags dominates the composition. Although Hassam suggests an atmospheric setting in this picture, the exaggerations implicit in the drawing and the vigorous brushwork, which deny depth and emphasize surface, carry this painting beyond Impressionism into a newer style suggestive of Expressionism. Fittingly, Paul Durand-Ruel, the man who introduced Impressionism to America, paid honor to Hassam with an exhibition of the flag paintings at the close of the War.

PLATE 32

OLD LONG ISLAND
LANDSCAPE
1920

Oil on canvas
55½" x 73" (140.9 cm x 185.4 cm)
The American Academy of Arts and
Letters, New York

The brilliant surface manipulation of pigment that is the prominent characteristic of the *Flag Series* paintings of 1916 to 1918 was an intermediate step in Hassam's late stylistic development away from realism toward a much more decorative use of color than he had ever before employed. Undoubtedly, the Armory Show of 1913 had impressed Hassam with the vast array of possibilities for experimentation open to the artist, despite his feeling that "so much [modern art] is obviously insincere and on the fool-fringe of the Fine Arts. . . ." Even conservative realist painters like Robert Henri were becoming aware of the new color theories, such as those proposed by Hardesty G. Maratta, and drastically altered their palettes. While there is no evidence that Hassam was ever inclined to follow such "scientific" theories, his awareness of modern tendencies in art cannot be doubted. This awareness surely contributed to the boldness, even the audacity, of certain color arrangements, such as the bright cadmium reds and the pure ultramarine blues that dominate the flag pictures.

Hassam's postwar landscape paintings partake of this new-found freedom to experiment with color. Unlike his earlier works, these new pictures do not seek to approximate the light of nature in an "optically correct" way. Often, as in *Old Long Island Landscape*, his palette was set in an extremely high tonal key. In this arbitrary disregard for naturalism, Hassam displayed a pronounced attachment to color for its own sake, which, when combined with the broad, mannered brushwork one finds in this Long Island subject, renders the painting an object in its own right more than a picture of something in nature. Distortions in drawing, which had become pronounced in the flag pictures, also attend Hassam's later work. Even when painting the human figure in a relatively straightforward manner, as in *Mixed Foursome (First Tee, Maidstone Golf Club)* (Museum of Art, Munson-Williams-Proctor Institute, Utica), 1923, the drawing is attenuated to the point of distortion.

Bibliography

Adams, Adeline. *Childe Hassam.* New York: American Academy of Arts and Letters, 1938.

Baur, John I. H. *Leaders of American Impressionism.* Exhibition catalogue. The Brooklyn Institute of Arts and Sciences, 1937.

Boyle, Richard J. *American Impressionism.* New York: New York Graphic Society, 1974.

Britten, James. "The Ten and the Academy," *American Art News,* (April 1915).

Buchanan, Charles L. "The Ambidextrous Childe Hassam," *International Studio,* (January 1916).

Buckley, Charles E. *Childe Hassam: A Retrospective Exhibition.* Exhibition catalogue. The Corcoran Gallery of Art, Washington, D.C., 1965.

Caffin, Charles *American Masters of Painting.* New York: Arno Press, 1902.

Clark, Eliot. "Childe Hassam," *Art in America,* (June 1920).

Corn, Wanda M. *The Color of Mood: American Tonalism.* Exhibition catalogue. Fine Arts Museum of San Francisco, 1972.

Cortissoz, Royall. *Catalogue of the Etchings and Drypoints of Childe Hassam, N. A.* Exhibition catalogue. New York, 1925.

Czestochowski, Joseph S. "Childe Hassam: Paintings from 1880 to 1900," *American Art Review,* (January 1978).

De Witt M. Lockman Papers, Archives of American Art, Smithsonian Institution. Microfilm File No. 503.

Eliasoph, P. *Handbook of the Complete Set of Etchings and Drypoints of Childe Hassam.* New York: 1933.

Hassam, Childe, "Twenty-five Years of American Painting," *The Art News,* April 24, 1928.

Homer, William I. *Robert Henri and His Circle.* Ithaca and London, 1969.

Hoopes, Donelson F. *The American Impressionists.* New York: Watson-Guptill Inc., 1972.

Hunt, William Morris. *Talks on Art.* New York: Dover, 1875.

James, Henry. *The Painter's Eye.* Cambridge, 1956.

Mather, Jr., Frank Jewett. *Retrospective Exhibition of Works by Childe Hassam, 1890–1925.* Exhibition catalogue. Durand-Ruel Galleries, New York, 1926.

Morton, Frederick W. "Childe Hassam, Impressionist," *Brush and Pencil,* (June 1901).

Novak, Barbara. *American Painting of the Nineteenth Century.* New York: Praeger, 1969.

Pousette-Dart, Nathaniel. *Childe Hassam.* New York: 1922.

Richardson, Edgar P. *Painting in America, The Story of 450 Years.* New York: T. Y. Crowell, 1956.

Robinson, Frank T. *Living New England Artists.* Boston: Garland Publishers, 1888.

Steadman, William E. *Childe Hassam.* Exhibition catalogue. University of Arizona, Tucson, 1972.

Stebbins, Jr., Theodore E. *American Master Drawings and Watercolors.* New York: Harper & Row, 1976.

von Saldern, Axel. *The Triumph of Realism.* Exhibition catalogue. The Brooklyn Museum, 1967.

White, Israel L. "Childe Hassam—a Puritan," *International Studio,* (December 1911).

William Preston Harrison Papers. Archives of American Art, Smithsonian Institution. Microfilm File No. 599. Letter to W. A. Bryan, 27 June 1924.

Zigrosser, Carl. *Etchings of Childe Hassam.* Exhibition catalogue, with an appreciation by J. Alden Weir. Frederick Keppel and Co., New York, 1915.

Index